THIRD EDITION

Life Prep

for homeschooled teenagers

A PARENT-FRIENDLY CURRICULUM FOR TEACHING TEENS ABOUT CREDIT CARDS, AUTO AND HEALTH INSURANCE, MANAGING MONEY AND BECOMING DEBT-FREE WHILE LIVING THEIR VALUES

Cardamom Publishers

Barbara Frank

Published by:

Cardamom Publishers
P.O. Box 743
Janesville, WI 53547-0743

Visit www.CardamomPublishers.com

Printed in the United States of America

Book design by FMD Inc.
Cover photo © 2003 by Sarah Frank

Mortgage charts courtesy of bankrate.com
Cover banner and images on pages 69, 70-75, and 80 used with permission © 2017 Shutterstock

ISBN 978-0-9742181-9-9

Library of Congress Control Number: 2017941108
Library of Congress Subject Heading: Home schooling, Budgets—Personal, Teenagers—Education, Home schooling—Curricula

To Sarah, who made *Life Prep* a necessity.
To Peter, who made additions to *Life Prep* a necessity.
To Mary and Joshua — Thanks for letting Mom write.
To Tim — Thank you for everything.
I am greatly blessed!

In loving memory of the Shellberg sisters

Table of Contents

The supreme end of education is expert discernment in
all things—the power to tell the good from the bad,
the genuine from the counterfeit, and to prefer the
good and the genuine to the bad and the counterfeit.
—Samuel Johnson (1709-1784)

Preface to the Third Edition

In 2003, my husband and I published *Life Prep for Homeschooled Teenagers* just as our oldest (and most intrepid) child was preparing to leave home. It was with mixed emotions that I shared with other homeschoolers the projects and reading material I used to get our daughter ready for life on her own, because while I thought she was now well-prepared to "leave the nest," I had no way of knowing for sure how it would go.

Fourteen years later, three of my little birds have long-since left home. All of them were on their own by age 20-22:

♦ Our eldest daughter lived in Chicago for many years after leaving home just before she turned 20. She chose not to attend college and has a good part-time job and a successful online business that she has run for years. She is now married and lives in another large city with her husband, where they own a house with a huge garden.

♦ Our eldest son graduated from college with highest honors … and sizeable student loans (despite our opposition). He married a fellow student (who had also amassed a lot of college debt) a few weeks after graduation. Both he and his wife have worked very hard, and we are proud to say they recently paid off all of their college debt. They have two children and own a house in a major Midwestern city.

♦ Our youngest daughter graduated from technical college with an associate's degree and worked as a police officer and then a legal secretary. She married a young man she met at tech college (who turned out to be a fellow homeschooler) and is now a stay-at-home mother to their baby girl.

Our adult children are doing very well indeed, and we thank God for that. We also believe that their success shows that homeschooling works (all of them were homeschooled through high school). Including *Life Prep* in our high school curriculum should also get some credit, as our kids have succeeded on their own with no financial assistance from us since they left home.

Since we first published *Life Prep*, personal economics has changed quite a bit, especially with the advent of debit cards, online banking, and a tremendous number of Web sites that help us to become wise consumers. The Affordable Care Act (ACA) also changed the face of health insurance as we had known it. Thanks to the economic ups and downs we've been through over the past 14 years, it's more important than ever to prepare our teens to live on their own before they leave home.

Hence this third edition of *Life Prep for Homeschooled Teenagers*. I've rewritten and expanded much of this curriculum to reflect the many changes in our economy since 2003:

- I've added two terrific books to the Reading List: *The Treasure Principle* and *George Muller: Man of Faith and Miracles.*

- The new "Work or College?" section includes information to help you determine if your teenager is "college material." Given the tremendous increase in college costs over the past 14 years, you can't afford to miss that section. Another new feature of that section shows you and your teen how to research potential careers to determine which ones are financially viable.

- There is a completely new section called "Borrowing Money, i.e. Debt." It includes three new projects: the Debt Penalty Project, the Debt Calculator Project and the Student Loan Project.

- Another new section, "Bank Accounts," includes three more new projects: the Checking Account Project, the Debit Card Project, and the Bank Safety Project.

- The Financial Freedom Project has been completely updated to reflect current economic realities and prices.

- The Health Insurance Project has been updated to reflect changes due to the ACA without eliminating the basics of health insurance (now that the ACA's future is in question).

- Other details and specific prices throughout the curriculum have been updated to reflect the current economy.

The dramatic growth of the Internet over the past 14 years has made it easier than ever to use *Life Prep* with your teenagers. Back in 2003, many of the resources listed in this curriculum had to be obtained by searching through used book stores or public library used book sales. Now it's quite easy to buy older or out-of-print titles online and have them delivered to your door. That's a great blessing to busy homeschooling parents.

Life Prep for Homeschooled Teenagers is intended to help parents prepare their teenagers for life on their own. But as you work on it with your teen, I hope it will also prepare you for the emotionally challenging yet necessary assignment of nudging your teen "out of the nest." May God bless you and your teenagers as you enter this exciting new stage of your lives.

Barbara Frank
February 2017

Introduction

What is *Life Prep for Homeschooled Teenagers?*

It's a curriculum that teaches teenagers skills and values they'll need in the adult world they're about to enter.

It walks them through processes like....

- researching a place to live
- figuring out health insurance
- understanding credit
- learning about basic investing

.... with an attitude of prudence, and a goal of minimizing debt.

It also reviews concepts they'll need for....

- getting along with family, friends, coworkers and clients
- finding a spouse
- living their values, and making sure those values are reflected in their work

.... and helps them reflect on the principles you've taught them since they were small.

Literature and mathematics are important, but so is getting ready to take on the adult world. I designed this curriculum for my own teenagers so they would have some preparation for living on their own. They worked hard and learned a lot, and are now independent young adults. I hope that *Life Prep for Homeschooled Teenagers* helps you prepare your own homeschooled teenager for life "out of the nest."

The need for
Life Prep for Homeschooled Teenagers

Homeschooled teenagers tend to be independent and self-motivated. Unwilling to see the traditional American high-school-then-straight-to-college trajectory as the Only Way to enter adulthood, many have plans instead to travel or start their own businesses, buy a house or get married. Some may even want to do one or more of those things in addition to attending college. But unlike their traditionally schooled peers, they aren't as willing to postpone their planning until after college graduation. They come out of homeschooling ready to tackle life.

In the meantime, their parents have been so caught up in the many details of raising and homeschooling a family that they're just starting to realize how little time to homeschool is left. There is still so much more real-life knowledge to share with their teenagers before they start full-time work or college. Their teenagers are talking about their plans for the future, but they don't even know how to handle credit or buy a car.

If those young people end up owning homes or businesses at a young age, they will need to have learned about credit and debt so that loans and mortgages are not foreign concepts. Daniel Pink, author of *Free Agent Nation,* a study of the rising trend of self-employment in America, notes that an increasing number of self-employed people were homeschooled. He believes that trend will continue and grow, because homeschoolers tend to be more self-directed and motivated than their traditionally-schooled peers.

Financial experts lament that American high school students graduate knowing little or nothing about personal finance. That should not be true of homeschoolers. We have the time and the ability to send our teenagers out into the world prepared to support themselves.

As we consider how soon our teenagers will be ready to leave the nest, we may also feel the need to review the values and ethics we've been teaching them, formally and by example, since they were small. Whether dorm life or the world of work awaits them, we know their values will be challenged. We will feel better if they have recently reviewed those precepts that are so important to their well-being.

Look at the world around you, and especially at the adults you know. How many of the problems they face have resulted from either not knowing how to handle money or not knowing how to get along with others? Those two areas seem to be difficult for many people. Teenagers will receive more future benefits from learning how to handle money and how to get along with people than from taking high school courses like Business Law or Western Civilization. So, while we've covered many subjects over the years, now is the time to cover the ones we really want to send them off with:

- how to live the values they've been taught
- how to get along with others in family and work settings
- how to handle money, credit and even wealth
- how to deal with difficulties in life

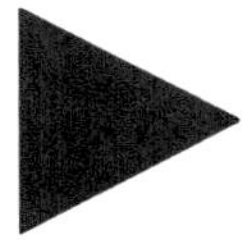

The genesis of
Life Prep for Homeschooled Teenagers

I designed *Life Prep for Homeschooled Teenagers* to cover those bases. I first developed the *Life Prep* course while homeschooling my then-16-year-old daughter. We only had one more year of homeschooling left, and there were still so many things I wanted her to know before she went out into the world.

I remembered how ignorant my husband and I felt when we bought our first house at age 22. We didn't understand how mortgages worked, and had no idea of what we were signing at the closing. We had to trust our attorney and the realtor. I thought then that someone should have prepared us for this in high school.

But we were never taught about such practical things in high school, and many high schools today continue to neglect financial education. While school officials often accuse their oldest students of having "senioritis," often seniors are just biding their time until graduation because what they are learning about is not useful.

One of my goals in homeschooling my children was to give them the opportunity to learn useful things and gain useful abilities. That goal gained a sense of urgency as our homeschooling years drew to a close.

Beyond providing financial literacy, I also wanted one last crack at delivering some worldview to my daughter. A review could not hurt, and this was my last chance to make her read something. So I made a list of books for her to read that reflected our values. They were books that I had read in the past, and that had impressed me with their authors' common sense, their views, and in a few cases, their genius.

So for both my daughter, and my son who followed her a year later, the last year of "homeschool high school" involved the usual subjects (Literature, Advanced Math, etc.) plus all the life skills and good reading I could squeeze into their days. Since one was work-bound and the other was college-bound, some of the reading and activities differed. But I did my best to include the most useful information for them, with consideration of their goals for the future.

The components of
Life Prep for Homeschooled Teenagers

Life Prep for Homeschooled Teenagers consists of three components: a section called "Work or College?," the Reading List, and a group of seven sections that include projects. All of these feature resources chosen with an eye to preparing our teens for adult life.

"Work or College?" is a small section with some very important information. College costs (tuition, room and board, and books) have increased over 1100% in the last 30 years, even as the median wage in America has stagnated over that same time period. As a result, there are millions of young people today who owe five- and six-figure student loan debt while earning minimum wage because they can't find jobs in their majors. They are basically debt slaves, unable to even imagine raising a family or buying a home someday. "Work or College?" will help your teenager avoid that fate by helping you determine if he or she is college material, and then help them find a career that is likely to pay off in terms of the cost of their training.

The Reading List includes books that will help our teenagers think about issues that they'll face when they're out in the world. Ethics, values, how to treat others and how to behave in different situations are all covered.

Within the Reading List are books that transmit Sir John Templeton's views on ethical investing, Sue Bender's joy upon rediscovering the value of work, and Dale Carnegie's timeless advice about getting along with others at work and at home, as well as many other wonderful books about different aspects of adult life.

Some of the books on the Reading List have a Christian viewpoint, others do not, but all of them transmit traditional values that seem near extinction in today's society. These values are not promoted by American media (indeed, they are more likely to be denigrated these days), so it's important to provide our teenagers with one last review of them before they leave home.

The remaining seven sections include projects that teach our teenagers about the kinds of things most of us had to learn through the School of Hard Knocks. Credit, rent, mortgages and budgeting are among the topics included. Step-by-step instructions allow the parent to make assignments to the teenager with a minimum of preparation on the parent's part. The main job of the parent who uses *Life Prep for Homeschooled Teenagers* is to obtain needed materials, be available to answer questions, and in some cases, provide Internet access.

The themes found in
Life Prep for Homeschooled Teenagers

The themes you'll find throughout *Life Prep for Homeschooled Teenagers* are sorely neglected by our society. For example:

Traditional values and ethics in the workplace

The Enron debacle and many other examples of corporate financial mismanagement, and even crime, illustrate the need for ethical behavior in the business world. Raiding pension funds, treating employees like consumable commodities, and stealing time and goods from employers are often considered to be merely the costs of doing business nowadays. Today's children need to be taught about fairness, honesty and the Golden Rule, so that their advent into the business world can bring about change. Homeschoolers must not miss the opportunity to teach such ethics because they ran out of time. They must make the time before their children leave home.

Financial knowledge, frugality and a cautious attitude toward unnecessary debt

We are living in unprecedented prosperity, according to the media. Indeed, huge houses and luxury SUV's are everywhere, it seems. People are buying and consuming an incredible array of material goods, while borrowing the money to pay for them. But many of these same people are drowning in debt. Bankruptcy and foreclosure rates are climbing. It's quite apparent that many adults don't know how to handle money. The lives they lead may look good on the outside, but are characterized inside by fear and worry. How can you live a good, productive life or have a happy marriage if you're consumed with anxiety about your increasing indebtedness? We owe it to our children to send them out into the world educated about debt and its pluses and minuses, as well as knowing how to handle money. Many of the projects you'll find here will do just that.

Christian worldview as it relates to families, work and money

The need for such a worldview is easily demonstrated by the decline of true family values (values that preserve the existence of the traditional family) in recent years, as evidenced by the high rate of divorce and the dramatic increase in illegitimacy in this country. While some of the books on the reading list are not specifically "Christian books," all of them reflect traditional values rooted in Christianity. Whether our teenagers go to college or start working full-time, they are sure to be exposed to ideas and attitudes that directly contradict what they've been taught. One last review of those values will send them off with the perspective they'll need.

How to use
Life Prep for Homeschooled Teenagers

You will find this book to be parent-friendly. As you get ready to use *Life Prep* with your teenager, your prime responsibility is the purchase or borrowing of materials. The books and resources in the Reading List have all been published or reprinted in recent years, and can be found in many places, including:

- retail and used bookstores
- mail-order and Internet booksellers
- library used-book sales
- at your public library or via interlibrary loan

The Reading List lends itself to the same format as any other high-school level subject your teenager may have studied already: she reads the assigned work, and then reports back to you orally or in writing so you can be sure she understood what she read. Essay questions are also provided for one book, *Your Money or Your Life* (see Appendix B).

Life Prep for Homeschooled Teenagers consists of three components: Work or College?, the Reading List, and Projects.

The projects in the Project List have been laid out, step-by-step, so that you can easily assign a project without doing a lot of groundwork. Some of the projects do require Internet access. If you don't have a home computer, or if you have one but it is not Internet-accessible, you can find one to use at most public libraries.

Customizing *Life Prep* for your teenager

Most experienced homeschoolers have learned to use curriculum as a tool, picking and choosing the areas needed by their specific child. They may not use a book starting at page one, but instead begin with the areas of greatest interest to their child, or with the areas they think their child needs to study most.

You can easily use *Life Prep for Homeschooled Teenagers* that way. Concentrate first on the areas most important for your teenager to learn. For example, if she can talk of nothing but that cute new Mini Cooper she wants (and especially if she expects you to pay for it), start with the Car Projects.

Consider also your teenager's plans for the future. If he already knows he doesn't want to go to college, you can omit the College Application Essay Project. If he's itching to get a place of his own, assign the Rent and Utilities Projects early on, so he understands exactly what moving out will cost him. (The sections "Instructions for Parents of the Work-bound Teenager" and "Instructions for Parents of the College-bound Teenager" provide specifics about what to include for the teenager who knows where he's going.)

Take into account what experience your teenager already has. If she's a pro at planning meals for the family, you won't need to spend as much time with the Food Expense Project as will those whose teenagers have never helped in the kitchen.

Most importantly, think about your own experiences since becoming an adult. In what areas do you wish you'd been more prepared? Dealing with credit? Buying a house? Understanding health insurance? You'll teach a subject better if you feel strongly about its importance.

Look at your own high school experience. Was it worthwhile? Why or why not? Did it prepare you properly for adult life? What do you want to do differently with your teenager? Getting such things clear in your mind may make you decide that certain projects in this book are especially important for your teenager. Think about what you have learned the hard way as an adult that you would like to teach your teenager about now. Chances are it's covered in this book. Whether you sat clueless at the closing of a home purchase, or still don't fully understand your taxes, now is the time to get it straight in your head while preventing your teenager from ending up in your position. Some of the best learning is learning together.

Don't be afraid to add to *Life Prep for Homeschooled Teenagers*. If there's a book you've read that has had a major influence on your attitude toward life and how you live it, add it to the Reading List. You'll have a great time discussing something that means a lot to you, and your teenager will not only learn from the book, but also learn a few new things about you.

**...Car Project,
...Rent and Utilities
Project,
...Food Expense
Project,
...Credit Card
Project,
...Health Insurance
Project**

How long does it take to do
Life Prep for Homeschooled Teenagers?

Like homeschooling, this curriculum should be geared to the individual student. Whether you choose to use every resource listed in this book, or pick and choose among them, depends on three factors:

- ◆ time constraints
- ◆ your teenager's past experiences
- ◆ your teenager's future plans

Time Constraints

First, how much time do you have to work with? Find the scenario below that most resembles yours:

*Your teenager is just beginning his last year of
home education:*

There's a time limitation here. How much time, realistically, can he devote to *Life Prep*? Consider the rest of his studies, his outside activities, and how often he works, if he is employed. Consider also, how important is it to you that he learn (or review) certain values and skills before he leaves home? Pick the areas most important to you and make time for him to study them.

*Your teenager has a few years to go before
he finishes homeschooling:*

You have a nice chunk of time to work with; make the most of it. You can assign work on a project-per-month and/or book-per-month basis, and accomplish a lot before he finishes his home education. As stated earlier, some areas will be especially appropriate at certain times. Capitalize on his interests and he will absorb far more of the material.

Your teenager is just beginning his teen years:

Start by occasionally assigning one of the books on the Reading List. Later on, as he matures, you can assign more reading and projects, gearing them toward his areas of interest or need.

Once you've determined how much time you have to work with, prioritize the books and projects listed in *Life Prep*. Start out with those you deem most important, so that you don't run out of time before you can assign them.

Determine also how much time you have to get personally involved. If you are homeschooling several other children, it may be easier for you to assign mostly reading, along with a few projects that don't require a lot of your involvement. Study the Project List and think realistically about which ones you can handle. While most projects were designed as activities for your teenager, some will require you to make information available by providing phone numbers or personal financial documents. Do you have the time for that?

Finally, don't feel that you must always assign every chapter of a book and every step of a project. If you're pressed for time, assign specific chapters of a book, those that emphasize something you really want your teenager to understand. Likewise, if the project you've chosen has a lot of steps, leave out those you think are not as important. For example, in the Car Purchase Project, if time is limited, just assign research on the particular model your teenager is interested in, instead of requiring research for several models.

Your Teenager's Past Experiences

Your teenager may have experience in some areas already, so those projects won't be as time-consuming for him. On the other hand, if he's weak in certain areas, you may want to spend more time on each step of a project, or on a certain book. For example, if he spends money recklessly, you'll want to take your time on the Budgeting and Credit Card Projects. If he tends toward anxiety, make sure he carefully reads and studies Dale Carnegie's *How to Stop Worrying and Start Living*.

Your Teenager's Future Plans

If he thinks he knows what he wants to do, assign your teenager the reading and projects that will benefit him most as they relate to his plans for the future. For more details, refer back to "Customizing *Life Prep* for Your Teenager."

How to Include *Life Prep* on Your Teenager's High School Transcript

To include *Life Prep* on your teen's high school transcript, you will need to determine how much time your teen spent on it, and for how long. If your teen worked on it a few times per week or less, count it as a half-credit. If your teen worked an hour or more a day on it, you can count that as one credit hour per semester. Include that credit on the transcript for as many semesters as *Life Prep* was used.

That's what I did on my teens' transcripts. I chose to use the phrase Life Prep, but you could also use other terms such as Personal Finance or Financial Literacy. (Don't over-think this too much; in my personal experience, college admissions departments are much more interested in ACT scores than transcript details anyways.)

Please note: The pronouns he and she are used randomly in this book, so that you don't have to see he/she and his/hers constantly. The use of he instead of she (or vice versa) should not be construed as a prejudice, but merely a convenience.

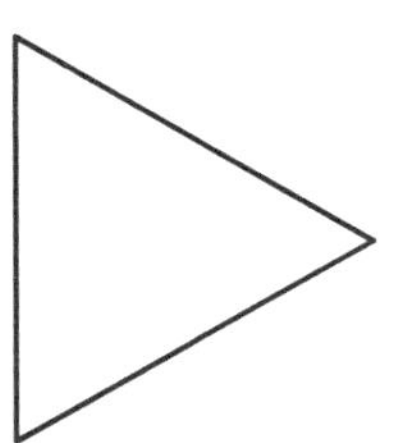

Work or College?

Work or College?

Background:

If your teen has already decided whether to go to work or to college after they finish homeschooling for high school, skip ahead to either "Instructions for Parents of the Work-Bound Teenager" (page 24) or "Instructions for Parents of the College-Bound Teenager" (Page 28) for help in choosing the reading assignments and projects they will need most.

If they haven't made that decision yet, you can help them by assessing whether or not they are college material. Being their teaching parent, you're in a unique position to do this, as long as you're completely honest with yourself.

In my book *Thriving in the 21st Century: Preparing Our Children for the New Economic Reality*, I offer some suggestions, based on my research, for determining whether or not your teen should go to college:

Before attending college became just another milestone on the path to adulthood, most people understood that college is intended for those who have the interest in and aptitude for higher learning. But today, even the president insists that every child should go to college.

As a parent, your priority isn't every child, it's *your* child. So the question is, should *your* child go to college?

Before you answer that, let's quickly review what you've read in this chapter. You now know that the greatest amount of job growth is predicted in areas that don't require college, that most kids who attend college don't graduate in four years and many don't graduate at all, that college is getting more expensive by the minute and that borrowing to pay those high college costs can have lifelong consequences. You also know now that having a college degree does not guarantee a high income…or any income at all.

Knowing these things, if you still think your child should go to college, please think hard about the following questions and whether you can answer "yes" to most of them:

- Is your child very intelligent and hardworking?
- Does your child have his/her heart set on a career that can only be accessed with a college diploma in hand?
- Of the careers that require at least some college education, is your child interested in one that offers the best return on the considerable college investment?
- Has your child thoroughly researched the chosen career, including talking to employers in the field to see what kind of education they require, and graduates in the chosen program to see if they're a) employed and b) satisfied?

- Is your child's choice of major/career one that's likely to be in demand by employers? (Just because a college offers a major doesn't necessarily mean that major is in demand by employers. There's no correlation between number of majors and number of available jobs.)
- Is your child's choice of major/career one that can be used in more than one industry? (Example: business administration)
- Is your child's choice of major/career one that will be difficult or impossible to off-shore (as opposed to an area of study that's currently being chosen by millions of smart young people from China and India)?
- Does your child's chosen college or university have a reputation for academic excellence?
- Will your child be able to graduate debt-free? In an economy where wages are stagnating and periods of unemployment or time between careers is common, living debt-free will be a major asset as well as a source of emotional peace.
- If your child will need some student loan funding, does he or she plan to earn a degree that is *likely* to help them earn enough to pay back their debt within a few years (there are no guarantees)?

Regarding the last question, keep in mind that the debt will have to be paid back during a time when wages most likely will continue to stagnate. As a result, college loan repayments could eat up the lion's share of your child's future paychecks.

"Yes" answers to most of these questions indicate that you have a child who is motivated to go to college and willing to do what it takes to earn a degree in a field with good prospects for personal satisfaction as well as employment. If you don't have enough money saved up for the entire four (or more) years, consider sending your child for two years of general education courses at a community college, after which your child can transfer to a four-year college. This is a time-honored plan, and for good reason: it saves a lot of money on tuition and room and board, plus you'll send a more mature person off to college. Also, if your child's chosen field of study will require graduate courses, the money you save by sending him/her to community college the first two years can help defray the cost of graduate studies later on.

If you can't answer "yes" to most of the questions listed above, consider whether college is really the answer for your child. Try to ignore the common wisdom of the 20th century that was drummed into your head, the refrain that insisted that the only sure route to success requires a college diploma, because times have changed.

Choosing a Career

Whether or not your teen has already chosen a career, there is an extremely valuable publication that will help you and your teen determine which careers have good prospects for the future and which do not. It's a U.S. government publication called *The Bureau of Labor Statistics Occupational Outlook Handbook*.

This book is updated annually and should be available at your local library. It's also available online; I highly recommend using the online version because it makes searching through this huge resource much easier. Just go to this Web site:

http://www.bls.gov/ooh

There you will find the handbook along with a variety of search suggestions including sorting results by pay, education required, and future prospects. There are even browsing functions that make it easy to find the occupations that are projected to be in the most demand in the future. Given our rapidly changing economy (thanks to automation and globalization), it's not enough to simply choose a career based on interest or aptitude anymore; your teen needs to consider whether a specific career is viable in the 21st century economy, especially if he will need to borrow money to obtain an education to prepare him for that career.

If your teen hasn't chosen a career yet, he can sift through the various careers listed and read up on those that sound interesting. If he has already chosen a career, this handbook will help him discern whether he's likely to find work in his chosen field and how much it will pay. The time your teen spends using this tool for research should count toward *Life Prep* class credit.

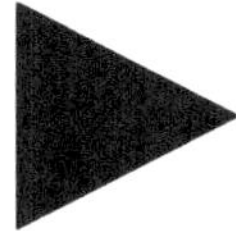

Instructions for Parents of the Work-Bound Teenager

If your homeschooled teenager plans to find a job as soon as she is finished with homeschooling, you will need to prepare her differently than if she were going to college, because work-bound teenagers face certain adult decisions sooner than their college-bound peers.

Where to start with the Reading List

A review of traditional values is certainly important for your work-bound teenager, and she will also need to read about how to get along with the people she'll be meeting out in the working world. In addition to those worthy topics, you should include a thoughtful study of how to handle the money that will be coming her way once she starts working full-time. For those reasons, make sure her assignments from the reading list include:

- Dr. James Dobson's *Life on the Edge*
- Dale Carnegie's *How to Win Friends and Influence People*
- David Chilton's *The Wealthy Barber*

Once she has read those three books, assign as many of the remaining titles as she has time to read.

Where to start with the Project List

All teens, whether planning on working or going to college first, need to understand how important it is to use debt prudently and only when necessary. So your work-bound teen should do the following projects first:

> ### The Debt Penalty Project (start at page 57)
> *This project will help your teen understand that using credit cards without paying them off each month is the same as paying a penalty on every single thing they buy.*
>
> ### The Debt Calculator Project (page 62)
> *Your teen will learn how to use a debt calculator, and then use that knowledge to learn about principal, interest and how to prepay a loan.*

The Financial Freedom Project (page 68)

This project uses the framework of a fable to illustrate how the decisions two teens make while they're young affect their futures, and make or break their dreams.

The Checking Account Project (page 85)

Your teen will learn how a checking account works and how to keep it balanced in this project.

The Debit Card Project (page 88)

Help your teen avoid the avalanche of fees that results with improper use of a debit card by assigning this project.

Full-time employment will bring with it immediate questions, such as how to fill out a W-4, and whether to sign on for the company's health insurance. Your teenager will handle those situations confidently if she's been prepared for them.

After she's been working for a while, and hopefully building up her bank account, the big question will arise: can she afford to get her own place? After completing the projects listed below, she'll be able to look at her options and discuss them with you knowledgeably.

Many of the work-bound teenager's needs are more pressing than the needs of those who are college-bound. That's why these projects should be next on her assignment list:

The Car Projects (page 131)

A car, typically a teenager's first major purchase, will be a necessity unless her job is within walking distance, or public transportation is available. Working through the Car Projects will make her first car purchase an informed one.

The Credit Card Project (page 95)

Your mailbox will fill with credit card offers for your teenager soon, if it hasn't already. A full-time income will be hard enough to keep from spending; the temptation of charging everything could send her into adulthood with a pattern of accumulating debt. Make sure you inoculate her by assigning this project.

> ### The Health Insurance Project (page 126)
>
> *As a result of the Affordable Care Act, young adults through age 26 can stay on their parents' health insurance policies. Nevertheless, you should still educate your teen about health insurance by doing this project. As an employee, she may be eligible for employer-provided health insurance; accepting or rejecting it should be an informed decision.*
>
> ### The Tax Project (page 143)
>
> *That first job brings with it questions of how many deductions to take, and how to file an income tax return. Prepare her for such eventualities with this project.*
>
> ### The Budgeting Project, Part 1 (page 111)
>
> *Your teenager will look at every paycheck as disposable income, unless she's been taught to plan for her needs and set aside money for them. This project will start her on that path.*

After your teenager has completed the projects listed above, it's time to cover those that will prepare her for eventually living away from home. Whether she plans to live on her own or get married, she will need to know the financial basics of establishing a household. These projects will provide her with that information:

> ### The Rent Project (page 103)
>
> ### The Utilities Project (page 109)
>
> ### The Food Expense Project (page 106)
>
> *Knowing when she can afford to move out will be an important issue for your teenager. Many people her age make grandiose plans for living in exciting places, but don't have a clue of what it would cost or whether they could afford it. These projects are particularly useful if your teenager has a destination in mind; they will force her to research her idea carefully. But even if she plans to hang out with Mom and Dad for the foreseeable future, she should be aware of what it would cost her to live on her own.*

Those projects should be followed up with:

> ### The Budgeting Project, Part 2 (page 113)
>
> *This project pulls together the costs determined by the Rent, Utilities and Food Expense Projects. The resulting total expense figure will provide your teenager with food for thought. It's better for her to have an idea now of what life on her own could cost, than to find out the hard way later on. Once she has experienced independence, moving back home because she couldn't handle it financially could be a very painful lesson, one that could have been avoided with some preparatory research.*
>
> ### The Mortgage Project (page 115)
>
> *Sooner or later, paying rent will seem pointless, and your young adult will want to buy a place to live. Working on this project now will provide the foundation for that big step down the road.*
>
> ### The Bank Safety Project (page 92)
>
> *This project will teach your teen how to find a good, safe bank in which to keep her hard-earned money.*

One more thing…

Most children have a savings account by the time they reach their teen years. It's a valuable tool that promotes saving money instead of spending it. But having a checking account is even more important, because it has practical value as well as teaching value. If you haven't done this already, establish a joint checking account with your teenager once she turns 16 (the minimum age in many states). Teach her how to balance it, and monitor her account's activity. She can write checks for giving, personal purchases and gifts. She may not use it much at first, but once she starts working full-time, it will be a necessity. The Checking Account and Debit Card projects work best if the student already has a checking account.

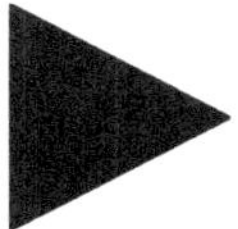

Instructions for Parents of the College-Bound Teenager

Whether a homeschooled teenager commutes to a local college, or leaves home to live at a public or private university, he suddenly takes on the freedom and the weight of making far more of his own decisions than he ever has before. Even if you raised a very independent-minded child, the abrupt change from living with his family to near-total freedom could be quite a jolt for him. Get him ready for college life with the following books and projects.

Where to start with the Reading List

Hopefully you, as his teaching parent, prepared him for the challenges to his beliefs that he'll face at college. He will encounter different viewpoints and worldviews, not just from his fellow students, but also from the instructors in positions of authority over him. He needs to be grounded in the values of your family so that he can rely on a secure belief system. This is doubly important if he goes away to college, because he won't have as many opportunities to discuss with you anything he's heard or has questions about, as he would if he attended a local college.

While all of the books on the Reading List are valuable, there are a few that are most helpful for the teenager who will soon be leaving your immediate sphere of influence. Before he leaves home, at a minimum he should have read:

- Dale Carnegie's *How to Win Friends and Influence People*
- Susan Schaeffer Macaulay's *How to Be Your Own Selfish Pig*
- Dr. James Dobson's *Life on the Edge*

Once he's read those three, assign as many others as you feel will benefit him. Make a special effort to include some of the books about financial freedom and investing, so he'll know how to handle all the money he hopes to make once he graduates.

Where to start with the Project List

All teens, whether planning on working or going to college first, need to understand how important it is to use debt prudently and only when necessary. So your college-bound teen should do the following projects first:

The Debt Penalty Project (start at page 57)

This project will help your teen understand that using credit cards without paying them off each month is the same as paying a penalty on every single thing they buy.

The Debt Calculator Project (page 62)

Your teen will learn how to use a debt calculator, and then use that knowledge to learn about principal, interest and prepaying loans.

The Financial Freedom Project (page 68)

This project uses the framework of a fable to illustrate how the decisions two teens make while they're young affect their futures, and make or break their dreams.

The Checking Account Project (page 85)

Your teen will learn how a checking account works and how to keep it balanced in this project.

The Debit Card Project (page 88)

Help your teen avoid the avalanche of fees that results with improper use of a debit card by assigning this project.

The Student Loan Project (page 80)

Unless your teen will attend college for free thanks to a full scholarship, a fully funded college savings account or a generous relative, he should understand how student loans work, how much debt he's likely to take on, and how much of a burden the repayment of that debt will be, by doing this project.

The College Application Essay Project (page 33)

The application essay is an especially valuable tool for the homeschooled teenager. This project will enable your future college student to submit an impressive essay along with his college application.

If your teenager plans to go away to college…

he'll also need to be prepared for the financial aspects of life on his own. Credit card companies will conspire to take a chunk of his money. Late-night pizza orders and other seeming necessities could wipe out what's left. He'll need to prepare for all sorts of financial temptations. That's why these projects should be at the top of his assignment list:

The Budgeting Project, Part 1 (page 111)

Most college students have to rely on a limited amount of money to get them through the school year. Using this project now will enable your teenager to "make the money last 'til May" once he's in college.

The Credit Card Project (page 95)

Colleges and universities have become the "happy hunting grounds" for credit card companies. They have found college students to be especially tempting, because they are usually short on cash and ignorant of sound money management. Don't let your teenager become one of the many college graduates who enter the adult world already saddled with massive credit card debt. Prepare him now with this project.

If your teenager will be commuting to a local or community college, or ***if he's taking a car with him when he goes away to college…***

assign the Car Projects in addition to those listed above.

The Car Projects (page 131)

Your teenager may not need a car while he's away at college, but most likely he will need to buy one just as soon as he graduates. Covering this project now will save him a lot of time later on.

Once they've been covered, you can then assign the remaining projects, which are important, though not as pressing.

If your teenager wants to live in an apartment while he attends college…

you will also want to assign these projects:

The Rent Project (page 103)

The Utilities Project (page 109)

The Food Expense Project (page 106)

The Budgeting Project, Part 2 (page 113)

> *These projects will be particularly valuable to him when he comes to the point where he must decide between a dormitory and an apartment. In the Rent Project, assign him only his intended universities' towns to research. His comparison charts should cover only properties near those universities.*

Once your teenager has completed the projects listed above, he can move on to:

The Tax Project (page 143)

> *Even if he doesn't plan to work while he attends college, your teenager will most likely need a job during the summers. He will have to fill out a tax return just to see if he's required to pay income taxes, or if he's entitled to a refund. This project will help him understand that process.*

The Health Insurance Project (page 126)

> *As a result of the Affordable Care Act, young adults through age 26 can stay on their parents' health insurance policies, whether or not they are attending college. So while this isn't a pressing issue, your teen will need to be educated about health insurance before he enters the adult world. So try to include the Health Insurance Project if you can.*

> ## The Mortgage Project (page 115)
>
> *It's a good idea to teach your teenager about mortgages, even if houses aren't in his immediate plans. According to the National Association of Realtors, the average age of a first-time home buyer in this country is currently 31, so you might want to prepare him now, while you have the chance.*
>
> ## The Bank Safety Project (page 92)
>
> *This project will teach your teen how to find a good, safe bank in which to keep his hard-earned money.*

One more thing…

Most children have a savings account by the time they reach their teen years. It's a valuable tool that promotes saving money instead of spending it. But having a checking account is even more important, because it has practical value as well as teaching value. If you haven't done this already, establish a joint checking account with your teenager once he turns 16 (the minimum age in many states). Teach him how to balance it, and monitor his account's activity. He can write checks for giving, personal purchases and gifts. He may not use it much at first, but once he goes to college, it will be a necessity. The Checking Account and Debit Card projects work best if the student already has a checking account.

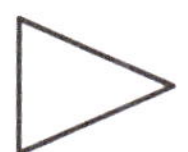

The College Application Essay Project

Background:

The college-bound homeschooled teenager should prepare for the college application process carefully and thoroughly. Her application won't land on the admission officer's desk complete with an "official" high school transcript, glowing reports from school counselors, and a list of high school activities and sports a foot long. Yet as a homeschooled student, she has many achievements and abilities that need to be brought to the attention of the college. Her application essay is an important tool for getting that job done.

The application essay will introduce your teenager to the admission officer. It should reflect her personality and her voice. As a homeschooler, she can use the essay to show that she can write well, but as one of hundreds or thousands of applicants to a given college, she can use her essay to reflect her unique personality. A well-written essay will make her stand out above other applicants.

Months before she actually has to submit application essays to her chosen colleges, she can practice the crafting of those essays, using actual essay questions from colleges and universities. You can guide her through that process by assigning her this project.

> **As a homeschooler, she can use the essay to show that she can write well ... she can use her essay to reflect her unique personality.**

Assignment:

Preparing to write practice essays:

____ Once your teenager knows of a few colleges she might be interested in attending, she should find each college's Web site, and access each one's application.

Assignment continued:

___ Your teenager should study each application to see if an essay is required from the applicant. If so, she should copy and save the essay requirements. This will give her some guidelines for writing practice essays.

___ Some college sites do not allow access to the application unless you're applying during that site visit. In that case, your teenager should request an application by mail.

___ If she cannot find very many essay requirements listed, she can do a search of other colleges or universities by using the phrase "application essay" in a search engine.

___ In addition to those essay questions your teenager has found, you can assign one or more essay questions from the following list of actual college-required topics:

What experiences have led you to choose your intended career field? (250 words)

Give an example of a "clever" mistake you have made, and explain how it helped you or others. (500 words)

Who has been the most influential person in your life? Why have you chosen him or her? (400-500 words)

Why do you want to attend this university? (400 words)

Are great leaders the product of their circumstances, or the result of their individual qualities? Make your case while describing the great leader of your choice. (500 words)

How would you like to be remembered after your life is over? (300 words)

Writing the practice essay:

___ After your teenager has chosen an essay topic, go over these general requirements with her:

- ◆ She must answer the question, and follow any other instructions or requirements.

- ◆ She should carefully develop her train of thought without going off on tangents.

- ◆ She should illustrate her statements whenever possible, with examples or descriptive phrases.

- ◆ She should not use up essay space describing accomplishments that will also be listed on the application itself.

- ◆ She should always remember her goal in writing an application essay: to show the admission officer who she is, thus personalizing her application.

- ◆ Every sentence must be her own; no plagiarizing.

- ◆ She should check any facts she may use, or quotations she includes.

- ◆ There must be no grammatical or spelling errors; a spelling program can't be relied on, as a phrase like "too years ago" will pass muster when it shouldn't.

- ◆ The word count of the essay should be very close to the length requirement.

- ◆ The essay should be neatly typed.

___ She should write a first draft, using an outline if you require one.

Assignment continued:

Editing and finishing the practice essay:

___ Once she finishes her first draft, you should go over it carefully, using the following parameters:

- ◆ Does she answer the question thoroughly but without rambling?
- ◆ Can you follow her main idea from beginning to end?
- ◆ Does her essay provide insight into who she is?
- ◆ Does she include specific examples, quotations or reasons?
- ◆ Does she avoid generalities and clichés?
- ◆ Does she run on, never getting to the point?
- ◆ Do you see any "padding" (extraneous material added to bring up the word count)?
- ◆ Do you see any spelling, grammatical or factual errors?

___ After making the changes you require, your teenager should do some revising of her own, clarifying anything that seems too vague, and making adjectives and verbs more descriptive where appropriate. She should then give it to you for final editing.

For Further Study

While reading the essay questions your teenager found at the beginning of this project, you probably noticed that the questions tend to fall into three categories: the "why did you choose this school/field of study?" question, the personal question, and the philosophical question. Assign as many essays of each type as you deem necessary.

For more specifics on writing college application essays, read *The College Application Essay* by Sarah Myers McGinty (available at www.collegeboard.com and most booksellers).

Reading List

Reading List

Background:

You may find that the reading level of some of these books, particularly the most recent, is rather easy. That's because their target audience is the average American consumer, whose reading level is not very high. But don't let that deter you from assigning such books, because your homeschooled teenager probably has plenty of other, more difficult books to read. Besides, you want to make it easy for your teenager to grasp these important concepts.

I required my teenagers to write essays about most of these books for the following reasons:

◆ an essay shows how well they read the book,

◆ an essay shows how well they understood the book's theme,

◆ sometimes they come up with really good insights that will make your day, and

◆ when you also have younger children to teach, assigning an essay to your teenager may be the most you can handle at that point in time.

The ideal, of course, is to discuss a book with your teenager, after *both* of you have read it. But if you decide to assign essays instead of discussion (or in addition to discussion), there are several forms you can use:

◆ assign a traditional book report

◆ assign a book review (includes more opinion backed up by quotes than a book report)

◆ give a title for the essay in order to provide a focus, such as "The Three Most Important Things I Learned From *Life on the Edge*"

◆ for a fact-filled book, assign your teenager to write a half-page summary of each chapter, then tie the summaries together with an introduction and a conclusion. I chose that option for my teenagers when they read *The Wealthy Barber*.

Note: Specific publishing information about books in the Reading List can be found in Appendix A.

Books About Living

George Muller: Man of Faith and Miracles
by Basil Miller

Why should your teens read this biography of a 19th century man who was a thief as a child but grew up to become a pastor and prayer warrior who devoted much of his life to "praying in" the funds he, his family and his ministries needed to survive? They should read it because Muller's life story vividly illustrates all the good things that can happen when you rely solely on God for your career and your physical sustenance. Muller kept a written record of his prayer requests and responses; this book is based on those records. This book will encourage your teens to trust God to guide them and support them throughout their lives.

Having Our Say: The Delany Sisters' First 100 Years
by Sarah L. Delany and A. Elizabeth Delany with Amy Hill Hearth

I had a number of reasons for assigning this book to my daughter. It is American history told by those who lived it, so it holds the reader's interest. It is also black history as told by two sisters who survived and even thrived despite the racism they faced during their very long lives. And it is inspiring to read about the love they felt for their family, the way their parents encouraged them to be the best they could be, and the love they had for each other, after being sisters for over 100 years.

The themes of faith and humor are woven throughout the book, in addition to plenty of life wisdom. It is so important for teenagers, who tend to be rather self-absorbed, to have the chance to view the world through the eyes of others. This book gives them that opportunity.

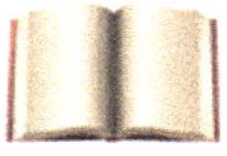

How to Be Your Own Selfish Pig
by Susan Schaeffer Macaulay

Don't be misled by the title of this book. Its subtitle is "…and other ways you've been brainwashed," and it's a manual for comparing worldly living to Christian living. Mrs. Macaulay is the daughter of Francis and Edith Schaeffer, Christian authors and founders of the L'Abri Fellowship Centers. The chapters in this book are based on discussions between members of Mrs. Macaulay's family and guests who came to L'Abri as a retreat from their personal troubles.

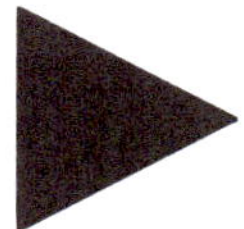

Books About Living:

Mrs. Macaulay's tone is friendly and frank, and while there are plenty of cartoons and humor used to bolster her points, the subject matter is serious. Despite its appearance, this is not a children's book. But the questions it asks about making choices, and the way it encourages readers to really think about their faith and decide what they believe, make it worthwhile, thought-provoking reading for teenagers. Their parents will enjoy it, too.

How to Stop Worrying and Start Living
by Dale Carnegie*

Yes, I know this book is old. To your teenager, it will seem positively ancient. But Dale Carnegie had a way of interspersing wisdom with tales from history that made his books very compelling, as evidenced by the many years they have been in print. While this book isn't overtly Christian, Carnegie never minces words about his Christian faith, and emphasizes frequently that faith is the antidote for worry.

This book would especially benefit the teenager with an anxious personality, but everyone can learn valuable lessons from reading it. Carnegie suggests how to remain relaxed while handling problems in both personal and business matters. Many of the true stories in this book recount what people went through in hard times in our country's history, and provide a bit of perspective for teenaged readers raised in these comparatively affluent times.

I Kissed Dating Goodbye
by Joshua Harris

This book is quite popular in some homeschooling circles. Harris believes that young people should steer clear of our society's tradition of dating, and instead remain friends. Should two people develop strong feelings for each other, he recommends that the couple remain pure while obtaining counsel from family, friends, clergy, and, of course, God, regarding the possibility of marriage.

The reason I assigned this book to my teenagers was not that I agreed with its

Before giving my teenagers Dale Carnegie's books to read, I assigned them to research and write a short essay about Carnegie. By learning about the man and his life experiences, they understood the times he was living in, and it gave them more perspective to bring to the reading of his works.

Books About Living:

premise that dating is wrong. In fact, I believe my husband and I were brought together by God via dating. However, this book contains so many good points about how Christians of the opposite sex should treat each other (with respect and concern, as brothers and sisters in Christ), and also about how the search for a marriage partner should be linked to one's relationship with God, that I made sure my teenagers read it.

Like other books of this type, *I Kissed Dating Goodbye* recommends going on outings with groups of people rather than as a couple. In his essay on this book, my son pointed out that since many people act differently in groups than they do one-on-one, you may not get to really know the person if the two of you are rarely alone. His dissent on that point showed me that he not only read the book but put some thought into his reading of it, which is the whole point of reading, isn't it?

Life on the Edge
by Dr. James Dobson

Of the many good books I used with my teenagers while doing *Life Prep*, this one is the best. If you've read anything else by Dr. Dobson, you know that clear writing and common sense are the hallmarks of his books, and this book is no exception. But what's really nice about *Life on the Edge* is that its intended audience is teenagers and young adults, and he addresses them directly.

Dr. Dobson discusses important subjects like choosing a career and a marriage partner, as well as just dealing with the ups and downs of life as a young adult in today's society. His Christian faith is always evident in what he writes, yet his practical advice is valuable for readers of any faith.

An especially valuable feature for homeschoolers is the addendum in the back of the book, where Dr. Dobson lists 38 principles that he has learned during his adult life. You can use these principles as jump-off points for discussions with your teenager, or choose some as essay topics.

When each of my teenagers finished *Life on the Edge*, I assigned the essay topic, "The Three Most Important Things I Learned From Reading *Life on the Edge*." Their essays made for interesting reading, and showed me that they had absorbed what they had read.

I also obtained the *Life on the Edge* video series for my teenagers, and that was definitely worth viewing. See Resources About Living for more details.

Books About Living:

Plain and Simple: A Woman's Journey to the Amish
by Sue Bender

Before she wrote this book, Sue Bender judged her life by her accomplishments. An artist and therapist with graduate degrees from Harvard and UC-Berkeley, she was also happily married with two sons, yet felt that there was still something missing in her life. A chance encounter with some Amish quilts resulted in a fascination with the Amish and their simple life of work and faith. She then went to live with the Amish for a short time as part of her quest to learn "how to live a good life."

The questions she poses in this book are even more relevant today than they were when this book was written in the late 1980s. Our young people are entering an adult world where more is always considered better, whether we are measuring work, money, material possessions or time. The frantic pace of American life, with its overabundance of choices, is often overwhelming. This book suggests that the Amish way of life can teach us a few things about slowing down and living one's faith.

The Shaping of a Christian Family
by Elisabeth Elliot

This is a valuable book, written by a godly woman who is greatly blessed with common sense. The author describes her upbringing in straightforward prose, seasoned with Scripture, poems, hymns, and excerpts from letters and journal entries written by her parents. There is no preaching here, just a narrative filled with insight that paints a wonderful picture of what a family should be. While all teenagers can learn from this book, I think it is especially valuable for young women, who need to counteract the dismissive attitude toward motherhood found in our society with a true-life example of what God-given power a Christian mother wields.

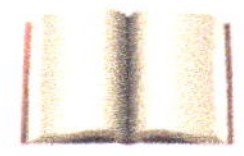

 Books About Living:

The Templeton Plan: 21 Steps to Personal Success and Real Happiness
by John Marks Templeton and James Ellison

How often do you get the opportunity to gain wisdom from a billionaire, and a Christian billionaire at that? In this book, investor and philanthropist Sir John Templeton uses examples from his own rags-to-riches story to provide readers with 21 steps to a happy and useful life. He does not suggest these are the only steps a person should take, but instead recommends that the reader start with these and add to them. He says people can fulfill their God-given potential "if we work continuously toward spiritual growth and better understanding of the virtues by which we should govern ourselves."

The way this book is organized, you can easily assign a chapter of reading at a time, and ask your teens to write a brief synopsis of each chapter as they complete it. That way, by the time they've finished reading the book, they'll also have a comprehensive guide to it, written in their own words. While each chapter does end with a summary or a set of review questions, your teens' take on it should include their personal insights and opinions about what they've read. They'll find plenty of satisfying food-for-thought in this book.

Resources About Living

Life on the Edge video series:

#1- "Finding God's Will For Your Life"
(on making life decisions wisely)

#2- "The Myth of Safe Sex"
(the subtitle "Self Control, Not Birth Control" says it all)

#3- " Love Must Be Tough"
(establishing and keeping healthy relationships)

#4- "The Keys to a Lifelong Love"
(establishing and keeping a loving marriage)

#5- "Emotions - Can You Trust Them?"
(making wise choices)

#6- "When God Doesn't Make Sense"
(dealing with difficulties)

#7- "Pornography: Addictive, Aggressive..."
(understanding the dangers of increasingly available pornography)

The *Life on the Edge* video series is a set of seven videotapes dealing with topics from the book of the same name. The book's author, Dr. James Dobson, gave several lectures before a group of nearly 200 students, and the lectures were taped for this video collection. The seven videotapes add up to almost six hours of viewing time. I highly recommend that you watch them first, or along with your teenager, so that you can handle any questions your teenager has, with full knowledge of what was said in the videos. Also, some of the tapes (especially #2 and #7) include candid discussions about sex and pornography, with which some parents may not be comfortable.

I watched all of the tapes, as did both of my teenagers. I found this series to be "candidly Christian" in tone, meaning that Dr. Dobson includes his Christian faith in everything he discusses, but doesn't shy away from talking about some pretty serious, and occasionally controversial, topics. That's a necessity in today's society; our teenagers are already witnessing sinful behaviors and attitudes, thanks to what passes for entertainment and news these days. They need plenty of perspective on these unfortunate happenings from a Christian viewpoint.

I highly recommend this video series for its common sense and Christian attitude about the issues and decisions our teenagers will face as adults. We were fortunate that our church has the collection in its library, so it was readily available for our use. At one time you could buy individual tapes or the entire series from Dr. Dobson's organization, "Focus on the Family." (See Appendix A for details.) This would be a sensible purchase for a homeschool group.

Books About Financial Freedom

Debt-Proof Living
by Mary Hunt

Mary Hunt's spending habits plunged her family deep into debt, and she eventually worked her way out of it by following principles she discusses in this book. Her informal style makes the information easy to understand, and she credits her faith for leading her out of financial bondage. Her take on credit card debt is to avoid it completely. This is a good reading assignment for the teenager who is susceptible to brand names and advertising.

The Treasure Principle
by Randy Alcorn

This brief but powerful book emphasizes that our money belongs to God, and that amazing things can happen in our lives when we acknowledge that fact and behave accordingly. Being generous (and having the financial freedom to do so) are key principles in this book. It will open your teen's eyes, and yours, too. Highly recommended!

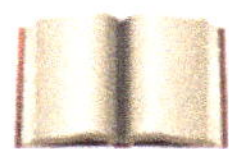

Invest in Yourself: Six Secrets to a Rich Life
by Marc Eisenson, Gerri Detweiler and Nancy Castleman

There is plenty of good information in this book about money management for self-sufficiency. The authors practice what they preach (Eisenson is also the author of *A Banker's Secret*), and they encourage frugality and common sense. Since the intended audience is adults with a fair amount of life experience, most chapters will not apply to teenagers. But there are several chapters that are worth your teenager's time; see the Mortgage Project, the Credit Card Project and the Car Projects for more details.

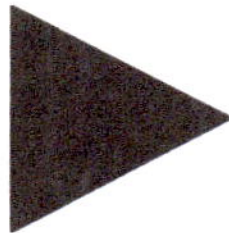

Books About Financial Freedom:

The Millionaire Next Door
by Thomas J. Stanley and William D. Danko

I found this book so interesting. I think all teenagers could learn a lot from it. Now I'm not saying we should instill in them a burning desire to live the life of the filthy rich; quite the opposite, in fact. *The Millionaire Next Door* is the result of 20 years' worth of research into how America's wealthy got that way, and the authors conclude that it's the result of three activities: working hard, saving money carefully, and living below your means.

This is the polar opposite of the message American youth receive today. Through the media, they are taught that appearances mean everything, and that if you want to be successful you must spend, spend, spend on clothes, cars, homes, and anything else that makes it look like you're living "the good life." However, the research done by Danko and Stanley shows that many of those who look like they've made it have actually harmed themselves financially by their accumulation of impressive purchases.

As the title of the book suggests, many millionaires live in average neighborhoods. They are mostly self-employed, often in non-glamorous lines of work such as manufacturing, pest-control services, or janitorial services. They don't believe in showing off (Danko and Stanley found "they believe that financial independence is more important than displaying high social status"), but they are more than financially secure. The combination of hard work and prudent decisions about how to live has assured them of financial security.

While this book doesn't preach, its emphasis on the success found by those who practice the three activities noted above makes it a welcome rebuttal to a culture obsessed with creating the impression of affluence.

(Please note that the 2010 edition of this book includes an updated foreword by one of the authors.)

Your Money or Your Life
by Joe Dominguez and Vicki Robin

This is a book written by independent thinkers. Since most homeschoolers are very independent-minded people, they might find a lot to like here. I know I did, so much that I assigned it to both of my teenagers, along with some essay questions I wrote for them (see Appendix B), to make sure they had picked up the important issues discussed in *Your Money or Your Life*.

In the United States, children grow up in a culture that promotes consumerism.

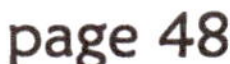

Books About Financial Freedom:

As a result, they often grow into adults caught up in a cycle of working to buy luxuries as well as necessities. Many people buy so many things that they end up stuck in jobs they don't like just to pay the bills they've run up. In *Your Money or Your Life*, Dominguez and Robin ask their readers to stop and think about whether their jobs reflect their values, and if not, how to remedy the situation.

The exercises in this book are intended for adults who have been earning money for a while. But the principles promoted in it are valuable for young people, too. Concepts such as finding a job that reflects your values, learning to discern between needs and wants, and deciding how many possessions are enough are certainly worth your teenager's contemplation.

There are many case histories discussed throughout the book, which help to illustrate the principles it promotes, and graphs and charts are used frequently to aid comprehension.

Most young adults are swept into the American way of working and consuming without having a chance to think about whether it is how they want to spend their lives. They eventually become so busy supporting themselves and their families that there's no time to think about what their lives have become. But teenagers getting ready to go out into the world are at a good place for thinking about how they want to integrate their values and their work. This book will start them on that path.

(Please note: most of this book is about useful principles, but the method the authors recommend for achieving freedom involves living frugally in order to save up a nest egg, and then living off the interest after investing it "safely" for a "modest" 5% interest rate. This is not currently possible, so focus on the principles in the book rather than the financial specifics, which naturally change over time.)

Getting a Life: Real Lives Transformed by Your Money or Your Life
by Jacqueline Blix and David Heitmiller

This is the follow-up to *Your Money or Your Life*. It describes the real-life experiences of people whose lives were changed by following the principles detailed in *YMOYL*. This can be used as supplemental reading for the student who finds *YMOYL* to be thought-provoking.

Resources About Financial Freedom

"Aiming for Financial Freedom to Achieve Your Dreams"
The Financial Freedom Project (page 68)

Like most teenagers, your child probably has big dreams and plans for his life. Many of them may sound a bit outlandish to you, but you probably had some pretty big dreams yourself at that age. No parent wants to rain on their child's parade, but the fact is that in today's credit-dependent society, many young people quickly lock themselves into credit card and student loan debt, thus sentencing themselves to years of working at whatever job they can find to keep their creditors from coming after them. Their dreams are soon forgotten because they're too busy just trying to make ends meet.

"Aiming for Financial Freedom to Achieve Your Dreams" is the written version of a conference workshop I have presented to homeschooled teens. It uses the framework of a fable to illustrate how the decisions two teens make while they're young affect their futures, and make or break their dreams. After you and your teen have both read it, discuss the fable, and be sure to share what your dreams were at that age, and how they were affected by the decisions you made.

"Affluenza" and "Escape From Affluenza"

These two videotapes were originally PBS specials, and they are definitely worth your teenager's time.

"Affluenza" is a documentary about the amount of conspicuous consumption going on in the United States, and whether it really makes people happy. Many of the people interviewed are proponents of the simple living trend, and they discuss how they gave up their pursuit of the dollar, and found more time to do things they enjoy, and to spend with loved ones.

There is much discussion about the ever-increasing pace of American life, and how one can step back and slow down. The effects of our consumptive lifestyle on the environment are also detailed.

"Escape From Affluenza" is the sequel to "Affluenza." Both documentaries are entertaining as well as informative, and some tongue-in-cheek humor keeps the tone light. At the time of this writing, you can watch them on www.YouTube.com. See the resource list in Appendix A for information on purchasing these films. Some libraries own them, so you may be able to borrow them from your own public library or through interlibrary loan.

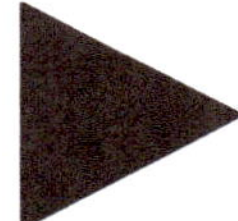

Books About Investing

Learn to Earn: A Beginner's Guide to the Basics of Investing and Business
by Peter Lynch and John Rothchild

You may not agree with some of Peter Lynch's views (for example, he'll never convince me that what Michael Eisner did for Disney was all good), but in this book you'll find that the mutual fund expert does a nice job of explaining how the stock market works. He wrote this for an intended audience of high school students, so it's not overly technical, and woven into it is a brief history of American capitalism that does not include the politically-correct negative spin on capitalism that you find so many places these days.

Teenagers who have expressed an interest in learning about investing, how companies work, or even running their own company someday will learn a lot from this book.

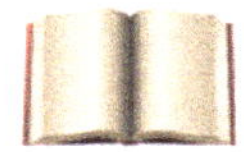

Ten Golden Rules for Financial Success: Riches I've Gathered from Legendary Mutual Fund Manager Sir John M. Templeton
by Gary Moore

If your teenager is interested in investing, here's a good book that will inspire thoughts of investing for wealth that is to be shared, not hoarded or spent only on oneself. Syndicated columnist Gary Moore details investing standards he learned from Sir John Templeton, famed investor and founder of the Templeton Prize for Progress in Religion. The beginning of the book takes an optimistic view of the economy, but so much has happened since this was written in 1996, that some of the information is dated. The reader will find, however, that the rest of the book is well worth reading. Moore discusses in detail Templeton's theories on tithing, having an attitude of concern for others, and investing to help others by stressing "the integration of spiritual principles and investment management."

For the young adult who is very interested in the specifics of investing, another good book by Gary Moore is *Spiritual Investments, Wall Street Wisdom from the Career of Sir John Templeton.*

Books About Investing:

The Wealthy Barber
by David Chilton

David Chilton's book provides an overview of personal financial management within the framework of a novel. He reports on the monthly meetings of a group of young people with their town's barber, a man who transformed his average-sized salary into wealth.

Each chapter describes one meeting, where the barber gives instructions for dealing with a specific financial issue, such as investing, taxes, mortgages, insurance and retirement. His prime emphasis is on taking 10% of your income and paying yourself first, then investing that money for long-term growth. Note that some of the financial news in this book is dated, but the basic principles are timeless.

Chilton's book was the basis for a PBS series 20 years ago. At the time of this writing, that series is available to watch at www.YouTube.com. While PBS no longer sells videotapes of that series, you can buy them at www.amazon.com or borrow them from many public libraries. Look for "The Wealthy Barber" and "The Wealthy Barber Returns." (Note: Videos might be the way to go if your teenager is an auditory learner.)

When I assigned this book to my children, I required them to write a half-to-one-page summary of each chapter as they read it. Once they finished the book, they added an introduction and a summary paragraph, in order to end up with a full book report. We also discussed any concepts they didn't understand as they read the book.

Books About The Working World

First, Break All the Rules
by Marcus Buckingham and Curt Coffman

The teenager with an interest in business, or an aptitude for managing people, should read this book. I had two reasons for assigning it to my son. After a long spell of wanting to work with computers, he suddenly decided he wanted a business degree, and I wanted to test his true interest level. Also, he spent a lot of time discussing how the employees where he worked should be treated (he felt management to be mostly indifferent to the concerns of his fellow workers and himself), and this book studies the methods of successful managers. In fact, it is subtitled *What the World's Greatest Managers Do Differently*.

Buckingham and Coffman (of the Gallup Organization) used 25 years of Gallup research into managers and organizations to determine what makes a successful manager, and they found that conventional management wisdom is often flawed. Their research revealed that the most successful managers succeed by treating people as individuals, instead of trying to mold them into employees who will fit into specific jobs. Rather than constantly emphasizing the possibilities of promotion, great managers help individuals develop their personal talents and strengths, work around their weaknesses, and find the right fit within their companies.

My son studied this book well, and wrote an excellent essay about it. His effort made it obvious that his interest in business was genuine. (Today, some 15 years later, he is the marketing manager for a large Christian publisher.) The book has a lot to say about how good managers work with people, and is useful reading for anyone who has management aspirations.

How to Win Friends and Influence People
by Dale Carnegie*

This book, in a nutshell, is about how to get along with people. One look at the world we live in tells us that this is much-needed information. This book is especially valuable for homeschooled students, because they will be heading out into a world where they may face some negative experiences and people that they missed out on by not attending public school.

Carnegie used true stories to illustrate lessons such as "Give the other person a fine reputation to live up to" and "You can't win an argument." The book is broken down by topics, so specific areas of help are easy to find.

Books About The Working World:

Most of the homeschoolers I've known find older texts to be as good and often better than newer texts, so the fact that this book was written in 1936 shouldn't deter anyone from reading it. It contains many basic truths about human relations that are timeless. Just the same, don't be surprised to find stories about such long-ago luminaries as Mary Pickford and Oliver Wendell Holmes.

While most of the book illustrates how to get along in social and business settings, there is a final chapter about getting along in marriage that sounds very antiquated. It suggests, for instance, that men should thank their wives for darning their socks (does anybody darn socks these days?), and that women should educate themselves about their husbands' line of work in order to remain interesting to them. Omit that section if it bothers you, or just discuss the "Seven Rules For Making Your Home Life Happier," which include the still-valuable rules "don't nag" and "don't try to make your partner over," among others. (Note: the final chapter was omitted from the most recent printing of Carnegie's book.)

Before giving my teenagers Dale Carnegie's books to read, I assigned them to research and write a short essay about Carnegie. By learning about the man and his life experiences, they understood the times he was living in, and it gave them more perspective to bring to the reading of his works.

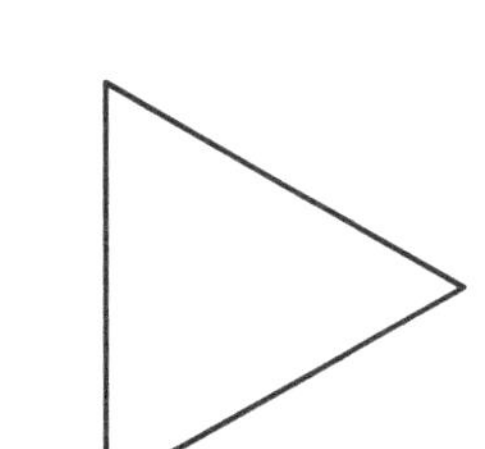

Project List

The Project List is a collection of practical exercises necessary to prepare teenagers for adulthood. The details of obtaining a place to live, food to eat, and a vehicle to drive are all available here, as well as how to pay for all those things without drowning in debt.

Personal Information Required

A few of these projects require you, the parent, to provide personal financial information, thus revealing your income and expenses. If you are a private person and don't want to share that information with your teenager, consider that the reality of what your family requires financially each month will help him understand just what it takes to raise a family these days. Such understanding may help him in his career planning as well as his eventual financial decision-making.

Internet Access Preferred

Several of the projects require Internet access. The ability to use the Internet for research is valuable for many reasons:

- it allows you to research prices and features of consumer goods quickly and easily, thus saving time while providing a lot of information
- many employers require potential employees to be experienced in Internet-based research; your teenager will need this ability to land many different types of jobs
- self-education is an important by-product of homeschooling, and the Internet is a primary self-education tool
- college-bound teenagers can save a lot of time by researching potential colleges online and taking virtual tours instead of making all those trips
- college-bound teenagers will find that once they've chosen a

college, much of the selection, admission and registration process will be conducted online.

If you do not have access to the internet, your teenager will have to use the resources of your public library. The reference librarian will be the best source of information.

Doing the Work

The teenager should do the work on all of the projects in *Life Prep for Homeschooled Teenagers*. He should be the one who:

- ♦ asks the librarian for help
- ♦ reads and photocopies the materials
- ♦ does the Internet research
- ♦ makes the phone calls

You will do him no favors if you take over those steps. They are a big part of the learning process.

Preparing for the Future

At first glance, some of these projects may seem like too much, too soon. For example, the Mortgage Project requires a lot of work. But more and more young people are buying residences these days; the National Association of Realtors says record numbers of people in their early 20's are buying places to live because low interest rates often make buying a place cheaper than renting it. Your teenager may be a homeowner sooner than you think.

Even if your teenager's first home purchase is many years off, learning about mortgages now will provide him with learning hooks, so that when he is faced with the situation later on, further information won't go over his head because he'll already have a general understanding of the topic.

So don't be afraid of projects with subject matter that you don't think will be needed for several years yet. Prepare your teenager now, and when the time comes to use the information, he'll be ready.

Choosing Projects

See "Customizing *Life Prep* for your teenager" (page 16) for details on choosing projects based on your teenager's future needs and plans.

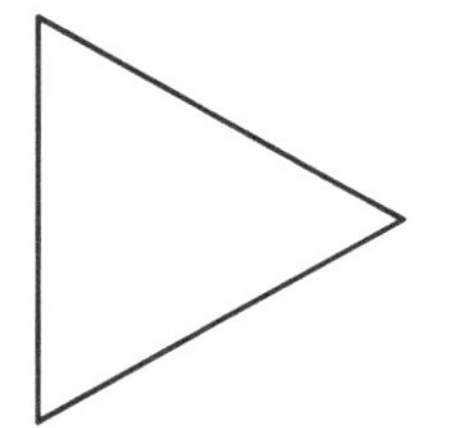

Borrowing Money, i.e. Debt Projects

Borrowing Money, i.e. Debt Projects

(Parents: have your teens read the following before they work on the Debt Projects.)

Background:

We live in a world where all is not what it seems.

For example, if you see a man driving a fancy car down the street or living in a mansion, you naturally assume he's rich. Sometimes that's true, but often it's not true. But if he's not rich, how can he afford to own such expensive things? The answer is that he borrowed money to buy them, and arranged to pay the money back little by little over the coming years. As long as he doesn't lose his job, he intends to pay all the money back. But until he does so, the fancy car or mansion is not technically his; in fact, if he fails to pay back the money on time, those items will be taken away from him.

So how does this affect you? As you become a self-supporting adult, you'll find that you can't afford to buy many of the things you need or want unless you borrow money to get them. Is there anything wrong with that?

The Bible, a book full of wisdom, states in Proverbs 22:7 that "…the borrower is servant, or slave, to the lender." What this means is, when you owe someone money, you give them control over your life.

For example, there was a young man who dreamed of becoming a missionary. After high school, he earned his bachelor's degree at a Christian college, borrowing tens of thousands of dollars in student loans in the process. Not long after graduation, he heard about the need for missionaries in a part of the world where he had long-dreamed of serving. But the missionary opportunity paid very little, and he had to earn enough to pay back his student loans. So he gave up on his missions dream and is stuck in the U.S. working at a job he hates. The debt he incurred controls his life choices now.

Here's another sad story: a young woman whose

"…the borrower is servant, or slave, to the lender."

parents insisted that she attend college (even though they couldn't afford to pay for some of it, much less all of it) borrowed the maximum student loan amount each year and also worked a part-time job in order to graduate from college in four years. She now works as a teacher. What's the sad part of the story? She fell in love with a young man and they were considering marriage, but when he learned that she owed over $75,000 on student loans, he told her he didn't want to start out married life with that kind of debt, and they broke up.

Student loan debt is just one kind of debt that's common in our society. Credit card debt is at record high levels, because racking up debt has become a lifestyle in our society. Many, many people are no longer free to follow God's call, or even to make their own choices. Their desire to spend more than they earn, financed by debt, has turned them into slaves.

But there is hope. Once you learn some truths about borrowing money, you can make wiser decisions than most people do. If you must borrow money, you can find the best deal for yourself and then commit to paying off the loan sooner than you're required to pay it off, saving yourself hundreds and even thousands of dollars of interest in the process.

You can also choose to live within your means and even save up a little money every time you're paid for your work. Having some money set aside means you don't have to borrow money for every little problem that comes up. It can even save you money, because when people live paycheck to paycheck (meaning they have no cash set aside), they often pay a penalty in the form of higher prices. We'll take a closer look at this concept, and the realities of debt in general, in the following projects.

The Debt Penalty Project

Background:

This project will help your teen understand that the regular use of credit can make everything cost more than it already does because of the interest rate charged on credit cards.

Assignment:

Read the following and answer the questions that are included.

Jessica went to the grocery to buy a few things, including meat for hamburgers. At the meat counter, she saw a sign stating that ground round cost $5.00 per pound, or $4.00 per pound for a 3-lb. package:

1) **The cost per pound in a 1-lb. package:** $ ______________________

2) **The cost per pound in a 3-lb. package:** $ ______________________

3) **If Jessica wants to get the best value for her money, which package should she buy?**

   ____

The best value would be the 3-lb. package, but it will cost Jessica more than buying the 1-lb. package.

4) **How much more?** $ ____

If Jessica is on a tight grocery budget, she may not have the extra money for the better deal and will have to pay the higher price per pound. She needs to learn to save a little cash from her earnings at her job so she can take advantage of good deals. With spare cash, she can easily take advantage of a money-saving opportunity like this. So she'll get the cheaper price, plus she can wrap and freeze what she doesn't use right away and it will be waiting for her in the freezer, saving time and gas when she needs more hamburger, and possibly helping her fight inflation if prices are rising and ground round is $6 a pound at the grocery the next time she shops.

Suppose Jessica not only doesn't have cash for the larger package of ground round, but she doesn't have any cash at all, and plans to put the groceries on her credit card, **on which she carries a balance**. This means she'll be paying about a 20% premium on that pound of ground round because the average credit card interest rate is 20%.

So how much will the 1-lb. package of ground round cost her if she puts it on her credit card?

5) **$5 × 120% =** __$__________________

Now compare that price to the price per pound she would have paid if she'd had enough cash for the 3-lb. package:

One pound of ground round on credit: $6
Per-pound price of ground round in 3-lb. package paid in cash: $4

6) How much can Jessica save per pound by paying cash for the ground round?

$______________

If you compare the per-pound prices, you should find that the credit card price is 50% larger than the cash price. That's a hefty penalty when you consider this is just one item on her grocery list. Imagine the penalty Jessica will pay by putting all her groceries on credit every time she shops!

Since Jessica doesn't save enough to keep a cash reserve for capitalizing on items like large packages of ground round at the best prices, she loses money by paying the higher price per pound, and then loses more money by paying interest on her little 1-lb. package of ground round. She's also spending more money than she has by putting her ground round on credit.

In a larger context, people who spend more than every dollar they earn often put their purchases on credit cards and pay the money back in monthly installments. This sounds reasonable until you remember that most people are paying over 20% in interest for the privilege, on every single thing they put on their credit cards: clothes, pizzas, vacations, you name it. And they pay that interest for years and years, if they don't make an effort to pay it off quickly. It's like paying extra every day of their lives. You'll learn more about this in the Credit Card Project.

Answers to questions can be found on page 153.

The Debt Calculator Project

Background:

This project will help your teen understand how debt calculators work, how the concepts of interest and principal in a loan work, and how prepaying on a loan can save interest costs.

Assignment:

Read the following and answer the questions that are included.

Christopher is a hard-working young man who restocks shelves at a home improvement store. When he's not working, he and a few of his friends have a band. They play local events for free and have gotten a good response from audiences. He's found some venues in other towns where they can perform for money, but he and his band mates need newer instruments and a van to carry them in when they go to gigs. However, none of them has enough money to buy these things.

He told his neighbor Mr. James of his plight, and Mr. James offered to loan Christopher $10,000 to pay for the instruments and a used van. Christopher was thrilled, and swore that he would pay the money back. Mr. James responded that he would require Christopher to sign paperwork to that effect, and that he would charge Christopher an interest rate of 5%; the loan would have to be repaid in five years.

To find out what Christopher's monthly payment to Mr. James will be, go to **bankrate.com** and click on **See all calculators** (under Popular Calculators).

Click on **Personal Finance** under **Calculators**.

Click on **Calculate your payment on any loan**.

Put in the loan amount, the loan term in years or months, and the interest rate. Then click **Calculate**.

1) **What will Christopher's monthly payment be?** $ __________________________

By signing a loan with Mr. James, Christopher will have to pay that amount back to Mr. James every single month for five years. If he misses a payment, Mr. James can take him to court. This is true of any loan you sign, by the way.

Now click on **Show Amortization Schedule**.

You should see a display that starts like this:

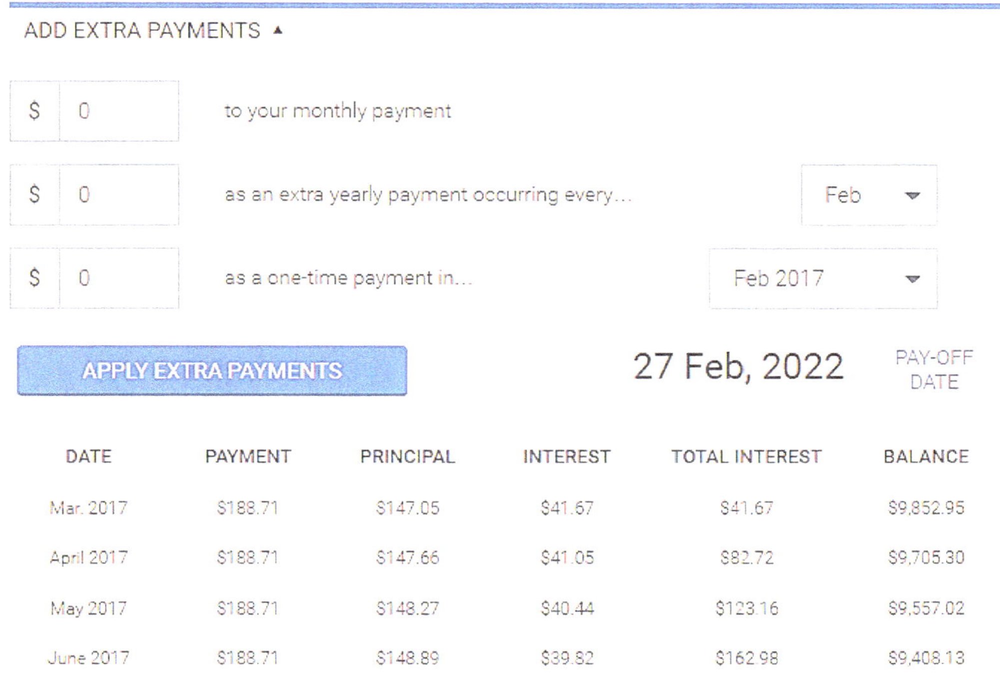

DATE	PAYMENT	PRINCIPAL	INTEREST	TOTAL INTEREST	BALANCE
Mar. 2017	$188.71	$147.05	$41.67	$41.67	$9,852.95
April 2017	$188.71	$147.66	$41.05	$82.72	$9,705.30
May 2017	$188.71	$148.27	$40.44	$123.16	$9,557.02
June 2017	$188.71	$148.89	$39.82	$162.98	$9,408.13

Assignment continued:

Note the **Pay-Off Date**, five years from now.

The first column, **Date**, lists every month for the next five years.

The second column, **Payment**, lists the same monthly payment amount for each of those months.

The third column, **Principal**, shows the portion of the $10,000 that Christopher will be paying back to Mr. James each month. Note that it doesn't stay the same over time but actually goes up. That's because the loan is front-loaded, which means that the lender receives most of the interest at the beginning of the loan.

The fourth column, **Interest**, shows how much interest Christopher will be paying each month. Note that it doesn't stay the same over time but that it actually goes down. Each month, Christopher's payment will include a little more principal (the amount he actually borrowed) and a little less interest (the price he pays the lender for the use of the money) until he finally pays it off in five years.

The fifth column, **Total Interest**, shows how much interest the lender, Mr. James, receives for the use of his money. Scroll down to the last entry.

2) What is the total amount of interest Mr. James will earn?

$ ______________________________

The sixth column, Balance, shows how much money Christopher will still owe Mr. James at any given point in time over the next five years.

Using this chart, determine the following:

3) Christopher borrowed $10,000 from Mr. James, but how much will he actually pay back over the five-year loan?

$ ______________________________

*****This is true of all loans that charge interest; you always end up paying back more, sometimes a lot more, than you borrowed.*****

That said, if you're allowed to prepay the loan, which means to make extra payments on the loan in order to pay it off early, you can save on interest charges.

For instance, suppose Christopher's loan money lets the band upgrade their instruments and gets them an old but decent van that allows them to do shows all over their state, and suppose the band becomes very popular, and before long they're earning thousands of dollars per concert. After a year, Christopher has easily set aside $5,000 to partially repay Mr. James. Let's see what will happen.

Under **Amortization Schedule**, see the section **Add Extra Payments**. Use the third box down to put in $5,000 **as a one-time payment** in the month two years from when the loan period began (the screenshot shows March 2017, so two years added to that is March 2019.) Click **Apply Extra Payments**.

AMORTIZATION SCHEDULE

ADD EXTRA PAYMENTS ▲

$ 0	to your monthly payment	
$ 0	as an extra yearly payment occurring every…	Feb ▼
$ 5,000	as a one-time payment in…	Feb 2017 ▼

APPLY EXTRA PAYMENTS

27 Oct, 2019   PAY-OFF DATE

DATE	PAYMENT	PRINCIPAL	INTEREST	TOTAL INTEREST	BALANCE
Mar. 2017	$188.71	$147.05	$41.67	$41.67	$9,852.95
April 2017	$188.71	$147.66	$41.05	$82.72	$9,705.30
May 2017	$188.71	$148.27	$40.44	$123.16	$9,557.02
June 2017	$188.71	$148.89	$39.82	$162.98	$9,408.13
July 2017	$188.71	$149.51	$39.20	$202.18	$9,258.62

The amortization schedule may look the same at first glance, but it shows a new pay-off date that is over two years sooner, and if you scroll down to two years from now, you'll see where that extra $5000 payment reduces the amount owed substantially.

Assignment continued:

4) Now look at the total interest paid, listed at the bottom. How much is it?

$ ___________________________

5) How much less is that than the original amount of interest Christopher would have paid back to Mr. James?

$ ___________________________

Being an increasingly famous rock star, Christopher may not care how much interest he saved by repaying some of the money to Mr. James a little early. But for most of us, saving over $450 is a very good thing!

Now let's look in another direction. Suppose Christopher borrows the money from Mr. James, he and his band mates upgrade their instruments, and they buy a van so they can drive to gigs. They find appreciative audiences, but they don't earn much in ticket sales. After a year or so, Christopher's band mates become discouraged. One guitarist leaves for the Army, another quits because his dad says he has to get a real job, and the drummer decides to join a different band. Christopher gives up and, since the van is in his name, uses it to drive to work instead of taking the bus.

But that's not the end of the story. Christopher's dream is gone, but he's still responsible for the money he borrowed from Mr. James. Every single month until the end of the five-year loan term, he will have to pay back $188.71. That may keep him from being able to save up money for a better car, from being able to leave home and get his own apartment, from taking some college classes or from buying his girl an engagement ring. Until he pays off the loan, nearly $200 of his earnings each month must go to Mr. James. That's part of the negative side of debt, in that it can keep you from doing things you want to do.

In our society, the reality is that some items are extremely hard to save up for, and you may need to borrow money to get them. For instance, if a nice, new house in your town costs $250,000, and you earn $12 an hour, it would take many, many years to save up for a house. A small house with a modest mortgage that you prepay might be a prudent answer if you need housing but don't want to tie yourself down to many years of very high payments. These are the kind of decisions you will have to make as an adult.

That said, people use credit far too often and get themselves into financial trouble as a result. The average American has:

- Credit card debt
- Student loan debt
- At least one car loan or lease contract
- Mortgage debt

Each of these ties down a portion of your monthly income for years. These debts can keep you from quitting a job you hate or taking a better job in another state. The more debt you take on, the more trapped you will become. Remember, the borrower is servant to the lender.

Answers to questions can be found on page 153.

The Financial Freedom Project

Background:

This project is different from the others in that no research is required. Everything your teen needs is right in this project. (You, however, will also be needed to share your experiences.) Its purpose is to demonstrate how the financial decisions your teenager makes in the next few years can have long-reaching effects. It will also encourage thoughts about what goals or dreams are important and their order of importance.

At the end of the section, there are questions for your teenager to answer, and some for both of you to discuss.

Assignment:

Your teenager should read the following fable and answer the questions at the end.

Aiming for Financial Freedom to Achieve Your Dreams

Everyone has dreams when they're your age. They may dream of travel, of a career, of marriage, or of all those things. But something happens to people as they become adults. Their decisions often make it impossible for their dreams to come true.

Nobody does this on purpose, of course. They just don't think of how the decisions they make will affect them down the road. In fact, many people don't realize how important the decisions they make when they're young really are.

I'll give you my own example. My husband and I married young, while we were still in college. Since neither of us liked paying rent very much, we decided we should buy a house. So, once we graduated and found

jobs, we saved up as much money as we could. We hardly ever went to movies or out to eat or to buy new clothes. That's how we were able to save up enough to buy our first house less than a year after graduation.

We were happy simply because that solved the problem of throwing away money on rent. We had no idea that house prices would go sky-high soon after, or that seven years later, we would make over $50,000 when we sold that house. Since we only paid $60,000 for it, that was a pretty good investment! It also allowed us to put extra money down on our next house, so we owed less money on it and could pay it off early. That's how we became debt-free. The decision to buy a house when we were 22 brought

us financial freedom in our 40s.

Now that was a good decision that led to more freedom for us. But sometimes young people make decisions that lead to less freedom. I want to illustrate that principle with a fable. Let's call it "A Tale of Two Teenagers."

A Tale of Two Teenagers

The two teenagers are Emily and Caleb. When our story starts, they're both sixteen. They're not a couple; they're just friends. They each live at home with their parents, so they don't need to work for food and a roof over their heads…not yet, anyway.

Their parents work hard to take care of their families, but they don't have a lot of extra money. So when Emily and Caleb complain that they need new phones, their parents have the same answer (what a coincidence!):

"Buy it yourself."

Emily wants the latest features on her phone. After some research, she finds a great deal on a cute little smartphone with plenty of data: only $40 a month and she can talk and text all day, but she has to sign a two-year contract.

Meanwhile, Caleb just wants something he can use to find out where his friends are meeting, or what time he has to be home. He decides to get a prepaid phone. He'll have to buy minutes for it every other month, and the minutes aren't real cheap, but after doing the math he realizes he can get a prepaid cell phone with a fair amount of minutes for talking and texting for $15 a month.

So now, at age 16, Emily has a monthly bill of $40 she must pay until she's 18 because she signed a contract, which is legally binding. Caleb has to pay $15 each month, but he can stop paying at any time without breaking a contract, because he didn't need one to get the prepaid phone.

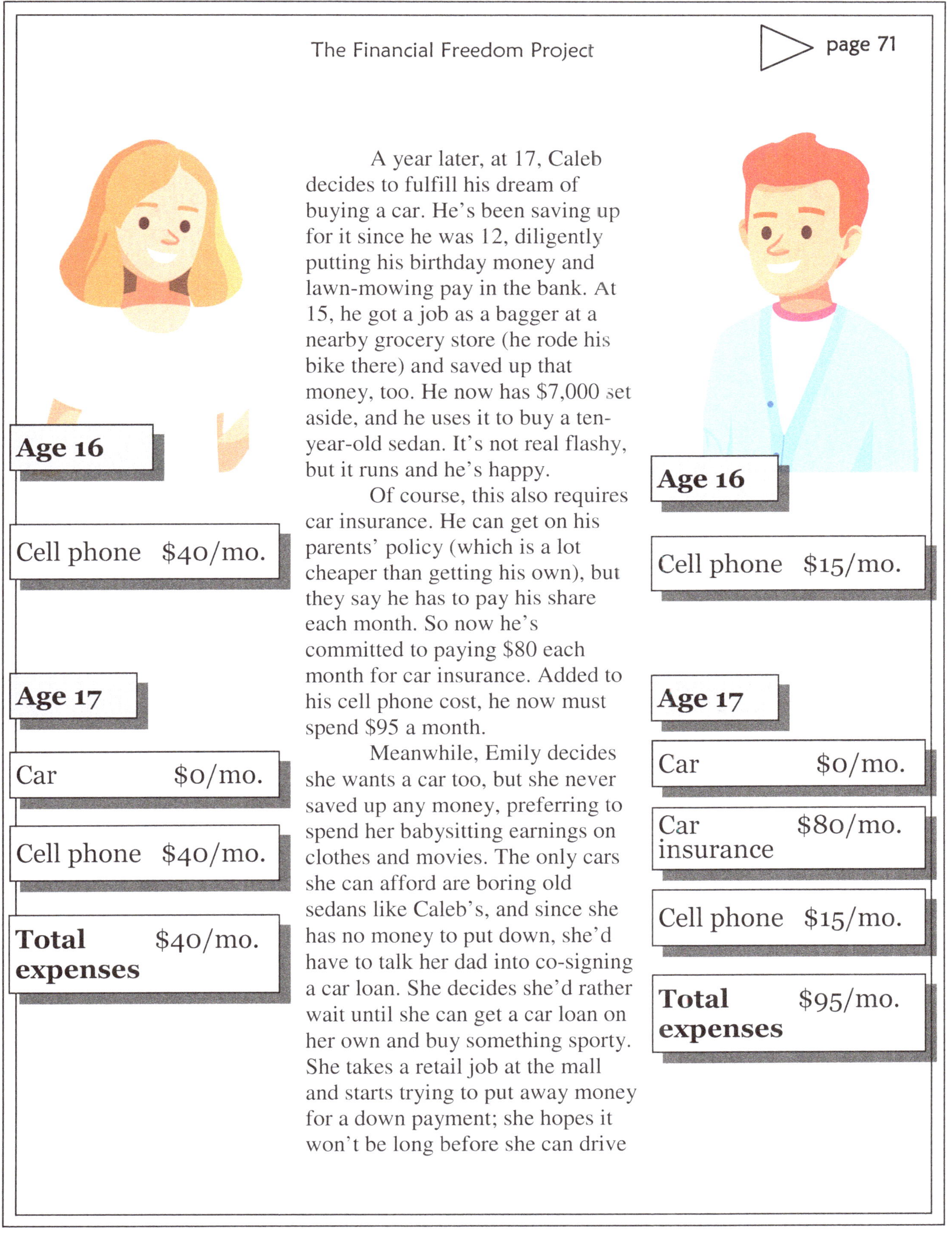

A year later, at 17, Caleb decides to fulfill his dream of buying a car. He's been saving up for it since he was 12, diligently putting his birthday money and lawn-mowing pay in the bank. At 15, he got a job as a bagger at a nearby grocery store (he rode his bike there) and saved up that money, too. He now has $7,000 set aside, and he uses it to buy a ten-year-old sedan. It's not real flashy, but it runs and he's happy.

Of course, this also requires car insurance. He can get on his parents' policy (which is a lot cheaper than getting his own), but they say he has to pay his share each month. So now he's committed to paying $80 each month for car insurance. Added to his cell phone cost, he now must spend $95 a month.

Meanwhile, Emily decides she wants a car too, but she never saved up any money, preferring to spend her babysitting earnings on clothes and movies. The only cars she can afford are boring old sedans like Caleb's, and since she has no money to put down, she'd have to talk her dad into co-signing a car loan. She decides she'd rather wait until she can get a car loan on her own and buy something sporty. She takes a retail job at the mall and starts trying to put away money for a down payment; she hopes it won't be long before she can drive

Age 18

Car loan	$230/mo.
Car insurance	$120/mo.
Cell phone	$40/mo.
Total expenses	$390/mo.

to work instead of taking the bus

Another year goes by. Emily and Caleb are now 18. Emily scores a newer smartphone and signs another two-year contract, while Caleb just keeps buying minutes for his phone every other month. They recently graduated from high school, but since neither one is sure what they want to do as a career yet, they both keep working.

Emily can now afford to buy her first car. It's an adorable, bright yellow six-year-old Mini Cooper; she fell in love with it as soon as she saw it. She puts down the $1,000 she's managed to save up as a deposit, and takes out a four-year car loan for $10,000, which means her car won't be paid off until she's 22. At 5%, her monthly payment will be $230 a month. Her car is worth more than Caleb's, which explains why she'll be paying $120/month for car insurance (compared to his $80 monthly car insurance bill).

So at age 18, Emily has committed to pay a total of $390 per month, while Caleb is still paying $95 per month.

At 19, both Emily and Caleb decide they are sick of working retail jobs and want to go to college. Caleb chooses to go to the local community college. He has figured out that if he goes for two years, he can earn an associate's degree in advanced imaging (giving people MRI's), which will eventually enable him to earn around $25 an hour, more than double what he's making at the grocery store. By going to community college, he can live at home to save money on room and board, and he'll use the money he's saved up from his job to pay for his classes and books.

Emily, however, is sick of living with her parents and thinks it high time she went away to college. Her parents cannot afford to help her financially, but she learns how to obtain financial aid, and takes out $20,000 in student loans to cover what's left after scholarships and grants (she won't have to start paying it back until after graduation). She buys new clothes for college (putting them on one of her credit cards), and happily drives her little yellow Mini off to college, where she plans to major in education in hopes of becoming a schoolteacher.

Two years pass, with both Emily and Caleb attending college full-time. They work during the summers, but it's hard to put away any money because of the other expenses they have. Caleb's car is starting to cost him money for repairs. Emily's car doesn't break down much, but when it does, it's really expensive because it's a foreign car.

Soon they are both 21, and Caleb graduates from community college with his associate's degree in advanced imaging. That summer, several of Emily and Caleb's friends decide they want to take a road trip and follow

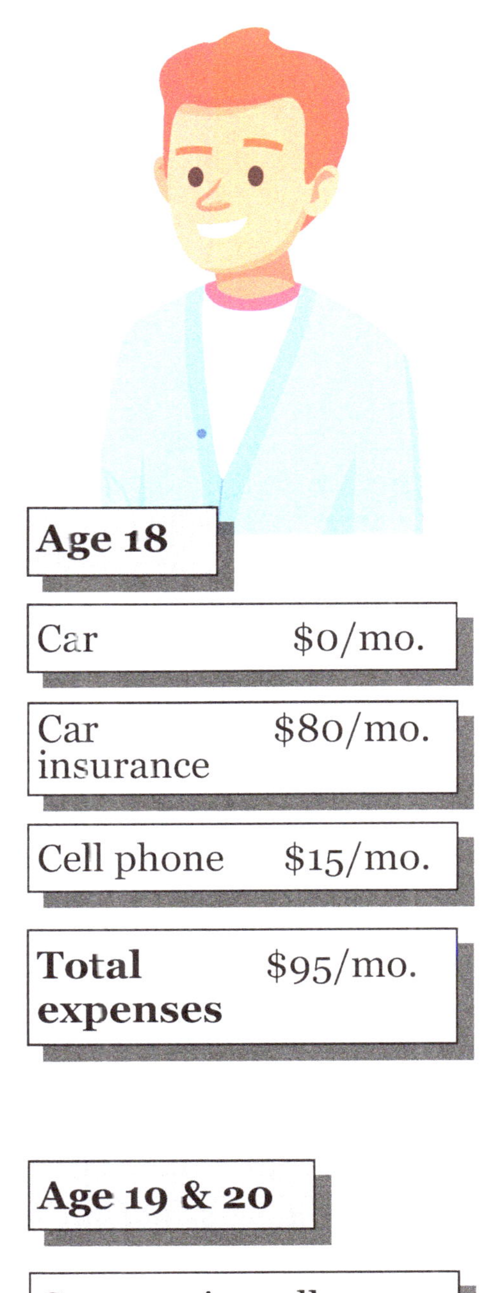

Age 22 & 23

Graduation

4 yrs. of $20 to 23K/year = $86,000 owed for student loans ($871/mo)

4 yrs. of credit cards = $15,000 owed
Min. payment = $375/mo.

Car insurance $60/mo.

Cell phone $40/mo.

Total expenses $475/mo.
($1346 when student loan payback begins.)

their favorite band around the country for a few months. Caleb can afford to take some time off before starting his new job, so he leaves his car at his parents' house (thus reducing his car insurance payment) and takes off with his friends for a road trip they'll always remember.

Emily would love to go along, but she must stay at her summer job in order to make her credit card minimums, car payment, car insurance payment and cell phone payment. Come fall, she continues to attend college full-time. Each year she takes out another student loan, and puts her books and other expenses (clothes, pizzas, music and movies) on her credit cards.

Meanwhile, Caleb comes back from his road trip happy and exhausted. He soon finds a job at a hospital, and is offered a starting salary of over $40,000 a year, or about $2,400 a month after taxes. With that kind of pay, he knows if he makes wise decisions about where to live and what to drive (his car is breaking down regularly by now), he can move out on his own and still put away money every month so he can eventually afford other dreams, like going on vacation to Europe or buying his own house. He has many options open to him.

Two years later, at 23, Emily graduates from college. Four years of credit card use has left her with over $15,000 in debt, and her student loan total is a whopping $86,000. She no longer has a car payment since she paid off her car a year earlier, and her car insurance dropped to $60 a month. But the minimum payments on her credit cards now total $375 each month (it will take at least 30 years to pay her credit cards off if she doesn't add to the balance by using the cards again), and nine months after graduation, her $871/month in student loan payments (for the next 10 years!) will have to be paid, so her monthly expenses will now come to $1,346 a month.

    This is money she must pay each and every month, even if she moves back in with her parents. Once she finds a job, she'll have the money to cover that, but will she have much left over to get her own apartment or a newer car? Nationally, the average new schoolteacher earns $38,000 a year, or about $2,500 a month after taxes. So Emily's debt has already eaten up more than half of her salary, once she gets a job. And since she has to make those payments each month, she can't take several weeks off like Caleb did after he graduated; she'll have to start working right away.

    If she continues to run up her credit cards, her minimum monthly payments will continue to go up, and she'll have to pay a higher interest rate on her next car loan (her yellow Mini is now 11 years old). After doing the math, she decides that for now, she'll have to move back in with her parents.

    Meanwhile, Caleb has been working full-time for two years. He now earns $45,000 a year, which translates into about $3,000 a month after taxes. This allows him to live comfortably in the small house he just bought (he qualified for a loan on a much bigger house, but decided he'd rather buy something less expensive and put the

difference in his savings account each month. He already has enough saved up for two weeks in Europe when his vacation time arrives.) He replaced his old beater with a much nicer car, and pays extra each month on his car loan so that he can get rid of the loan sooner.

Do you see how the decisions Emily and Caleb made when they were younger affected them at age 23? Emily's willingness to go into debt for everything severely limited her freedom to make choices. She missed out on the road trip because she had to work to pay her bills. The credit card and student loan debt she racked up during college will follow her for at least the next ten years, tying her to a regular job no matter what, and putting tremendous pressure on her should she find herself unemployed at some point. (Studies show that 20-40% of new teachers quit after their first year of teaching.)

On the other hand, Caleb's choices gave him freedom. He was able to go on the road trip, something he'll remember his entire life. At 23, he already has a house, a nice car, a bank account and an impending trip to Europe. Because he has no college or credit card debt, he'll be free in the future to have even more choices.

Even the little things make a difference. Emily's unlimited cell phone minutes got her accustomed to talking as long as she wanted, so she didn't switch to the prepaid phone, which would have saved her $25 a month ($600 over the course of her two-year contract). She got used to buying clothes and fun stuff with her credit cards while she was in college, establishing a pattern that she is not likely to give up, so her credit card debt (and monthly payment) will probably increase as she gets older.

Caleb's spending habits also established a pattern. By minimizing debt, he'll never be tied to a job he doesn't like in order to keep up with a large amount of monthly payments. He's been able to invest in a house (an appreciating asset in his area, meaning it goes up in value) without using up all his monthly income. With no college debt, he has total access to his entire salary, not just half of it like Emily has.

Money = Freedom   Debt = Bondage

The point of our story is that the decisions Emily and Caleb made as teenagers had lasting consequences on their adult lives and on how much freedom they would have. While both of them chose careers that are in demand (so they'll have something to fall back on no matter where they work), Caleb also chose financial freedom by making wise choices. In our society, the more debt you have, the less freedom you have. The more debt you have, the longer you will have to be tied to working full-time.

People who have financial freedom are able to work when they want to. They can take time off to travel or do missionary work. They can try starting their own business or building their own house. One homeschooled girl bought a corner of her parents' acreage and built her own house after taking a homebuilding course out East. She built the house and paid for the land using cash she'd saved up. Now she owns it all free and clear, and can be picky about when and where she works.

As you get older, you will have more choices, and the choices you make will affect you for many years. In order to make good choices, you need to educate yourself now about financial matters and about financial freedom (how to get it and keep it). The person who has financial freedom has found a way to achieve their dreams. As for the person who is in financial bondage because of their debt, they will never be free until they pay it off.

The rich ruleth over the poor, and **the borrower is servant to the lender.**
Proverbs 22:7 KJV

Questions:

(Please note that "Total expenses" refers to monthly commitments; of course, a person has many other expenses, as described in the Budgeting Project.)

1) What decision did the author and her husband make when they were young that benefited them later on?

2) How did they benefit from that decision seven years later?

3) How did they benefit from that decision twenty years later?

4) In the fable about Emily and Caleb, what was the first purchase each made, and how much did it cost each of them?

5) A year after that purchase, which one of them would come out ahead financially and by how much?

6) At 17, Caleb bought a car. What steps did he take to make his car purchase affordable?

7) Why was Emily unable to buy a car at age 17?

8) When Emily bought a car she liked at age 18, how much did it cost? Once she paid it off at age 22, how much had she actually paid for it?

9) Emily chose a newer, sportier car that cost more to insure than Caleb's car did. How much more did she pay to insure it over four years than Caleb paid to insure his over the same time period?

10) When Caleb decided to go to college, he made several wise choices. What were they?

11) When Emily decided to go to college, she made several financially risky choices. What were they?

12) What event in Emily and Caleb's lives demonstrated who was free and who was not? Explain your answer.

13) At age 21, what are Caleb's dreams? What are the chances he'll achieve them? Why or why not?

14) At age 23, Emily graduates from college. Can she take some time off after graduation for a trip? Can she afford to live on her own?

15) If at age 23, Emily and Caleb feel called into missionary work or some other form of service to their fellow man, will they be able to answer that call? Why or why not?

16) The habits we develop when we're young become an integral part of our adult lives. What habit did Caleb develop with regards to credit? What habit did Emily develop with regards to credit?

17) Using what you've learned about Emily and Caleb so far, write an epilogue to this fable, describing their lives when they are 30.

18) List the dreams you have for your life. What would you like to have achieved by the time you're 30? What wise financial decisions can you make now and in the next few years to help you reach your goals? Discuss this with your parents.

19) Ask your parents: Looking back over your life so far, which decisions that you made worked out best for you from a financial viewpoint? Which turned out to be financial mistakes? What would you do differently if you could do it over?

Answers to questions can be found on page 153.

The Student Loan Project

Background:

The cost of a college education has increased exponentially in recent years; according to the U.S. Bureau of Economic Analysis, it rose 137% between 2000 and 2015. Unfortunately, the average American family's income did not increase during that same time period. This explains why so many students borrow so much money to go to college now; in 2016, *U.S. News and World Report* stated that 70% of American college students have student loan debt, with the average 2016 college graduate owing over $37,000 at the time of graduation.

That debt must be repaid whether or not the graduate finds a high-paying job. That's why your teen's choice of career should be a profitable one if he plans to borrow money to attend college. But college admissions workers won't tell you this. In fact, most colleges, including many Christian colleges, consider student loans a necessary evil. (This is particularly unfortunate in the case of those students who are preparing to work in a church-related field, where the pay is not usually on the high end of the spectrum.)

Ultimately, it's up to the teen and his parents to decide whether borrowing large amounts of money in order to earn a degree is worth spending ten years to repay the debt. This project will help your teen get an idea of just how much money he might have to repay each month.

70% of American college students have student loan debt, with the average 2016 college graduate owing over $37,000 at the time of graduation.

 ## Assignment:

____ Go to the following Web site:

https://bigfuture.collegeboard.org/pay-for-college/loans/student-loan-calculator

____ Enter your expected graduation year and potential salary in the first two boxes. If you don't know the average starting salary in the career area you've chosen, you can look it up in *The Bureau of Labor Statistics Occupational Outlook Handbook*, which should be available at your local public library. You can also access it online at http://www.bls.gov/ooh

____ Fill in the boxes for Federal Direct Student Loans for Undergraduates, and also for Graduate Students if your chosen career field requires a graduate degree. Use the listed maximums if you haven't chosen a college yet. Otherwise, subtract your chosen college's estimated total fees (tuition, room, board, books and activities) from the amount of money you and your family can afford to pay for college each year to help you compute how much money you'll need to borrow.

____ If the borrowing limits on the Federal Direct Student Loans are not enough, you can also fill in the boxes for Perkins Student Loans (which can sometimes be cancelled if you become a teacher in a low-income school after graduation).

____ If those two options still don't offer enough money to help you pay for your choice of college program, fill out the boxes for other loans.

____ According to the *New York Times*, only 19% of full-time students in public colleges graduate in four years; most require six years. Consider whether you will need more than four years to graduate from college and therefore additional student loans. If so, fill in the boxes for "5th year."

____ Click the "Calculate" box.

Assignment continued:

___ You should see an estimate of:
- ◆ how much money you'll have to borrow,
- ◆ how much it will cost you per month to repay the loan over the ten-year period after graduation (whether or not you find a job that pays what you expect your chosen career field to pay), and
- ◆ an assessment of whether your potential loan burden will be "manageable," which is defined as not more than 10-15% of your estimated first-year income.

___ Talk to your parents about the estimated monthly cost of student loans that you may end up with, and see how they feel about it.

___ Compare your estimated monthly student loan cost to your expected monthly income after taxes. Will you be able to cover your other expenses (housing, food, insurance, phone, transportation, etc.) in addition to the loan payment each month? Will you be able to save a little money each month for emergencies? Will you be able to set aside money in a retirement plan?

___ Did you know that you'll have to repay those loans even if you drop out of college before graduation? So, for instance, if you drop out after freshman year, how will you repay the money you borrowed?

___ If you and your parents are not comfortable with this kind of debt, consider a career field that does not require a college education. If you and your parents are comfortable with borrowing the estimated amount so you can attend college, go to the next step.

___ Go to the following Web site:

https://fafsa.ed.gov/fotw1617/pdf/PdfFafsa16-17.pdf

___ This is the application you'll have to fill out if you intend to apply for any kind of financial aid for college. It should be filed as early as possible at the start of each calendar year during which you plan to attend college. However, your parents should have their taxes ready to be filed before you can complete the form, because you'll need some numbers from their tax form(s).

___ You will use this form to apply for scholarships and grants (which don't have to be repaid) as well as loans, so anyone who plans to attend college should fill out and submit this form each year of college.

___ You can have your financial aid information sent to up to four colleges, so fill out this form even if you haven't chosen or been accepted to a college yet. This will help you compare the financial aid packages offered at the different colleges to which you will apply.

___ This form can be submitted electronically, which will get your results quickly. But you'll have to set up an account first by going here:

https://fafsa.ed.gov

The combination of overwhelming student loan debt and a lackluster economy with many new college grads working at low-paying jobs because they can't find higher-paying jobs in their field has caused some young people to become hopeless and to even commit suicide because they don't see any other way out of what feels like endless years of servitude. Please read this article and in particular, read the comments that follow it.

http://alleducationmatters.blogspot.com/2010/08/suicide-among-student-debtors-whos.html

After that, consider whether your financial situation combined with your teen's choice of a major/career field could force your teen into similar circumstances.

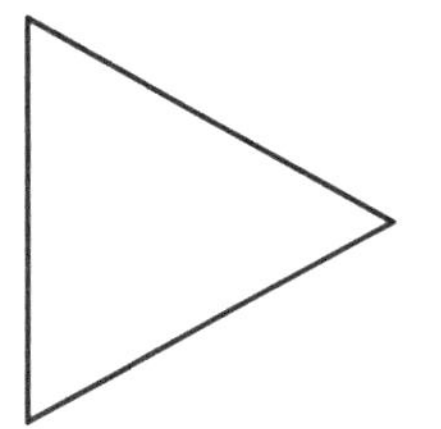

Bank Accounts & Credit Cards

Bank Accounts

It's possible to exist on a cash basis in the modern world, but it's very cumbersome whenever your payment must be mailed instead of being paid in person. That's why the use of a checking account makes it much easier to pay bills. At one time, we all wrote checks to pay our bills (some still do), but the advent of the debit card has made our transactions less cumbersome than ever.

That said, there are dangers in the use of the debit card. For that reason, teens need to learn about checking accounts and debit cards as soon as they begin earning their own money.

The Checking Account Project

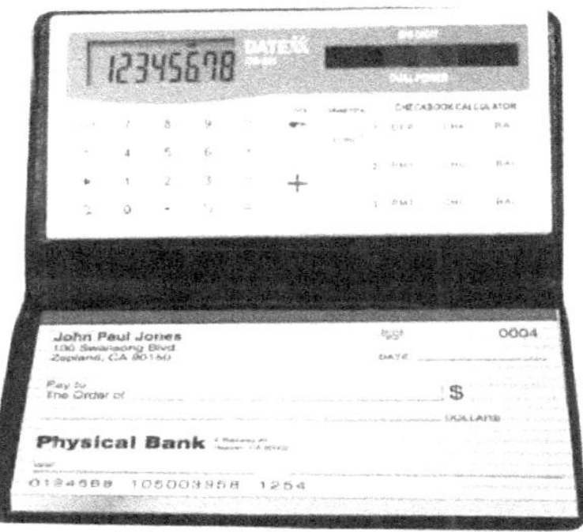

Background:

This project will help your teenager understand how a checking account works, and how to keep it balanced and accurate at all times.

Assignment:

____ If you don't already have a checking account and a debit card, go with one of your parents to their bank and set up both. Choose the no-fee checking account if possible; otherwise, get the best deal you can.

____ A checking account is a bank account that lets you take out money by writing checks or using a debit card for purchases. It's up to you to keep track of all activity in your checking account to insure that you don't overdraw your account, meaning you don't take out more than you have in the account. In order to do this, you'll need to use a check register. Your bank should provide you with one; you'll get more whenever you order more checks. Even if you don't intend to write checks, you should always use a check register. You can download a free check register here:

https://d2e70e9yced57e.cloudfront.net/wallethub/images/posts/14483/check-register-printable.pdf

Or, if you'd prefer to keep track of your checking account in Microsoft Excel, download this check register:

http://www.vertex42.com/ExcelTemplates/excel-checkbook.html

___ Every time you put money in your account, or take money out of your account, you'll need to write down or enter the transaction in your check register, noting the date, description and amount. If you put money into the account, you'll write it down on the next empty line and the amount deposited in the Deposit/Credit column. Whenever you write a check, take cash out at an ATM, incur a fee with the bank, or make a payment online, you'll write it down on the next empty line and put the amount spent in the Payment/Debit column. At the end of each line, either add the amount if it's a deposit, or subtract the amount if it's a payment, and then write down your new balance.

___ Let's practice by printing out a check register using one of the links provided and entering the following transactions:

- ◆ On January 1 you put $250 into your new account, noting that it is the starting balance.

- ◆ On January 2 you used your debit card when you spent $6.24 at Taco Bell.

- ◆ On January 2 you wrote check #101 to your mom to repay the $25.00 you borrowed from her a while back.

- ◆ On January 5 you used your debit card to buy $27.32 worth of music from Amazon.com.

- ◆ On January 8 your paycheck from McDonald's was direct-deposited into your account; it was $189.52.

____ Your check register should now look similar to the following:

Codes - ACH: ACH Payment | ATM: Cash Withdrawal | BP: Bill Payment | DC: Debit Card | D: Deposit | DD: Direct Deposit | SF: Service Fee | WT: Wire Transfer						
CHECK NUMBER/ CODE	DATE	TRANSACTION DESCRIPTION	(−) PAYMENT/ DEBIT	✓	(+) DEPOSIT/ CREDIT	BALANCE
	1/1	Starting Balance			250 —	250 —
DC	1/2	TACO BELL	6 24			243 76
101	1/2	MOM	25 —			218 76
DC	1/5	Amazon - music	27 32			191 44
DD	1/8	Paycheck			189 52	380 96

____ If your balance is not $380.96, go back and check to see where you went wrong and fix the register so that it reflects the correct balance.

____ Save this practice check register for the Debit Card Project.

____ Keeping your check register updated is a very important task, and a habit that you should develop right away.

____ Every month your bank will provide you with a checking statement, either by mail or on your bank's website. It shows all the activity that occurred in your checking account over the previous month. As soon as you can, make sure your check register agrees with the bank's records by reconciling your checking statement. There should be instructions on how to do this on your checking statement, or you can ask your parent to show you. It may seem like a nuisance, but you need to know exactly how much money is in the account at any given time so that you don't overdraw it and incur fees. Also, the bank occasionally makes mistakes and they're not usually in your favor; the sooner you find the mistake and notify them, the sooner they can fix the problem and give you back your money.

____ If your bank allows you access to your bank account online, you'll need a password for your bank's Web site. Do not share this password with anyone but your parents. Checking your account balance online regularly will help you keep track of your balance, but you'll still need to keep a register separately. The reason for this will be discussed in the Debit Card Project.

The Debit Card Project

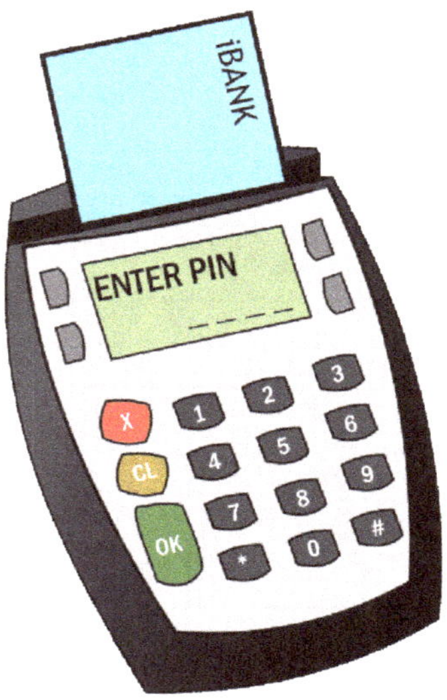

Background:

The debit card is one of the most convenient and dangerous financial tools a person can have. This project will teach your teen how a debit card works, and how to avoid racking up banking fees by using it properly.

Assignment:

___ Use the practice check register from the Checking Account Project and enter these new transactions:

- On January 8 you used your debit card to buy an iPhone on eBay.com for $203.87.
- On January 9 you withdrew $40.00 from an ATM at the mall.
- On January 9 you used your debit card to buy a movie ticket for $8.75.
- On January 9 you used your debit card to buy a drink and some popcorn at the movie theater for $9.33.

___ Your check register should now look like this:

Codes - ACH: ACH Payment	ATM: Cash Withdrawal	BP: Bill Payment	DC: Debit Card	D: Deposit	DD: Direct Deposit	SF: Service Fee	WT: Wire Transfer							

CHECK NUMBER/ CODE	DATE	TRANSACTION DESCRIPTION	(−) PAYMENT/ DEBIT		✓	(+) DEPOSIT/ CREDIT		BALANCE	
	1/1	Starting Balance				250	—	250	—
DC	1/2	TACO BELL	6	24				243	76
101	1/2	MOM	25	—				218	76
DC	1/5	Amazon - music	27	32				191	44
DD	1/8	Paycheck				189	52	380	96
DC	1/8	eBay.com	203	87				177	09
ATM	1/9	Cash	40	—				137	09
DC	1/9	movie	8	75				128	34
DC	1/9	movie - snacks	9	33				119	01

____ If your balance is not $119.01, go back and check to see where you went wrong and fix the register so that it reflects the correct balance.

____ Now, suppose you go online to check your bank balance, and you see that it is not $119.01, but instead it is -$20.99. Scrolling down, you see that you have been charged $35 overdraft fees for your last four transactions, for a total of $140.00 in fees. How can this be? When banks accept direct deposits, they usually put a little asterisk near the amount or put the word "Pending" nearby to show that the deposit is in the account, but you can't touch that money until the next day. Since you bought the iPhone on the very day your paycheck was deposited, you spent some of that money while it was still pending. As far as the bank is concerned, you spent money you didn't have yet, which overdrew your account on January 8.

____ To make matters worse, the next three transactions on January 9 (ATM, movie ticket, movie snacks) overdrew your account further, and resulted in three more overdraft fees for a total of four fees of $35 each.

Codes - ACH: ACH Payment | ATM: Cash Withdrawal | BP: Bill Payment | DC: Debit Card | D: Deposit | DD: Direct Deposit | SF: Service Fee | WT: Wire Transfer

CHECK NUMBER/ CODE	DATE	TRANSACTION DESCRIPTION	(−) PAYMENT/ DEBIT		✓	(+) DEPOSIT/ CREDIT		BALANCE	
	1/1	Starting Balance				250	—	250	—
DC	1/2	TACO BELL	6	24				243	76
101	1/2	MOM	25	—				218	76
DC	1/5	Amazon - music	27	32				191	44
DD	1/8	Paycheck				189	52	380	96
DC	1/8	eBay.com	203	87				177	09
ATM	1/9	cash	40	—				137	09
DC	1/9	movie	8	75				128	34
DC	1/9	movie - snacks	9	33				119	01
SF	1/8	overdraft fee	35	—				84	01
SF	1/9	overdraft fee	35	−				49	01
SF	1/9	overdraft fee	35	−				14	01
SF	1/9	overdraft fee	35	−				− 20	99

____ At this point, you don't have any money in your account (you actually owe the bank $20.99). If you try to use your debit card, the purchase will go through but you will incur another $35 overdraft fee.

Assignment continued:

____ It's likely that when you set up your checking account, the bank offered you a service called "overdraft protection," which you accepted. After all, it sounds good; the bank lets your purchase go through even though you don't have enough money in your account. But they charge you a hefty fee for the privilege. What you can do is opt out of overdraft protection. Then if you try to use your debit card when there's not enough money in your account, your card will be declined. However, if you write a check when you don't have money in your account to cover it, the bank will not pay it and it will be considered a bad check. You can be arrested for this. If you have overdraft protection, the bank will honor the check…and then charge you an overdraft fee. This is one reason why it's very important to keep your check register up to date.

____ If your checking account is a truly free checking account, you won't have to keep a minimum amount of money in it. But often checking accounts have minimum balances, and if you go below those balances, you will be charged another fee. Again, ***it's very important that you always know exactly how much you have in your checking account before using your debit card or writing a check.***

____ If you keep track of your checking account online but don't keep a check register (or don't look at it), you may forget that you wrote a check a few days ago, and when you go online and see your balance, you'll think you have more money than you actually have because the forgotten check hasn't gone through the bank yet. If you spend that money, and then the check arrives at the bank, you may find yourself being charged more fees. This is yet another reason why it's very important to check your account regularly.

____ If you keep track of your account online and you see a charge that you don't recognize, even a very tiny one, call your bank immediately. It's likely that someone is trying to use your debit card number (they may not have stolen your card but just randomly tried a number that turned out to be yours) to access your account. The bank will tell you how to proceed.

____ Always keep your debit card number to yourself; when you use it in public, block other people's view of your PIN as you enter it. When you use it online, make sure the Web site is protected; usually you'll see a padlock at the top, and the site link will begin with "https." This will help protect your account.

___ If someone uses your debit card to break into your account, they may empty it, and the bank is not required to replace the money. You're liable for $50 if you report it in the first two days, up to $500 if within 60 days, and there's no limit to your liability if you don't report the loss for more than 60 days. Even if you do report it promptly, it may take a few weeks to get your money back. This is different from credit cards; if someone steals your credit card and uses it to make purchases, you will not be held responsible as long as you report the theft as soon as possible.

The Bank Safety Project

Background:

This project will teach your teen something important while he helps out the family by performing a useful service.

Over the past decade or so, the FDIC has closed one or more U.S. banks at the end of some weeks. These closings aren't widely publicized, but they happen. No one wants to find out their bank is one of the failed banks, especially once it's too late to do anything about it.

Sometimes the banks are merged with other banks and the transition is seamless. But if that doesn't happen, the bank is closed by the FDIC and bank customers may have to wait to get their money back, which is very inconvenient. That's why no one wants their money in a failed bank.

Once your teen learns how to check the safety of any given U.S. bank, including your own, he'll know how to find safe banks, and can even look up this information for Grandma and Grandpa to make sure their bank is a good one, too.

The Web sites your teen will use in this project display reports that explain exactly what's going on in a bank, and where problems may be looming. Most teens won't want to read these reports, preferring just to look at the wrap-ups. Those who do want to read the particulars may be candidates for careers in accounting or investment banking. In either case, reading the reports and looking up unfamiliar phrases would be a good learning exercise for teens and parents.

Assignment:

__ The Federal Deposit Insurance Corporation (FDIC) is an agency that keeps tabs on U.S. banks to make sure they're in good financial condition. The FDIC has the power to close a bad bank, and will reimburse the bank's customers for up to $250,000 if it does so. However, it can take a long time to get your money back, so it's best to only do business with good banks.

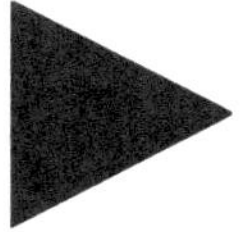

Assignment:

___ To find a good bank, you can use free online services that let you look up any bank and make sure it's not headed for a Friday night closing. These services study the financial situation of each bank and rate it based on performance and prognosis. In the economic climate of recent years, it makes sense to protect your hard-earned dollars by keeping track of your bank's safety rating.

___ Ask your parents for the name of their bank (or credit union). Then go online to this Web site:

http://www.bankrate.com/rates/safe-sound/bank-ratings-search.aspx

___ Enter the name of the bank (or credit union) in the box "Search by Name" and then click the button marked "See Results."

___ Click on the name of your parents' bank; you will see a long report. Note the number of stars the bank has been given by Bankrate.com; 1 star indicates a bank in bad financial shape, while 5 stars is a sign of a bank in excellent shape.

___ Now go to this Web site:

http://www.bauerfinancial.com/btc_ratings.asp

___ Enter the name of the same bank and click "Search!"

___ Note the number of stars that the bank has been given by BauerFinancial.com.

___ Some banks are in trouble because they made too many imprudent loans, but you can take a look at a bank's troubled asset ratio by going to this Web site:

http://banktracker.investigativereportingworkshop.org/banks

Assignment continued:

___ Search for the bank by name or by using the interactive map.

___ You will find a chart that shows how the bank's troubled asset ratio has compared to the national median for the past five years. Note its most recent ratio on the far right. It's best to use a bank with a troubled asset ratio well below the national median.

___ On the right side of the main page of this Web site, find the list of bank closings by year. Note how many banks have been closed this year. For comparison purposes, 157 banks were closed in 2010, 92 banks were closed in 2011, but only seven banks were closed in 2015.

___ With the knowledge you've obtained from these three Web sites, decide whether your parents' bank is a safe bank to use. Look up other local banks to see which ones are doing well, and which ones aren't. Share what you learn with your parents.

The Credit Card Project

Background:

How do you feel about your teenager having a credit card?

You may not have given this much thought yet, but before long, your son or daughter will be the recipient of a steadily increasing barrage of credit card offers filling your mailbox. If you don't teach your teens about credit and its advantages and disadvantages before then, you may find that they will consider these offers to be "free money."

That's a dangerous attitude to have; the high rate of personal bankruptcies in our country has its roots in adults who view credit as free money. Advertising encourages this attitude with slogans like "No Payments Until 2018!" With the debt of the average American credit card user now at over $15,000, it seems prudent for parents to teach their teens about credit. But some parents don't believe in using credit cards, and don't want to even touch on the subject with their teens.

A reader contacted me a while back and suggested that I omit the credit card project from the next edition of *Life Prep for Homeschooled Teenagers* because teaching teens about credit would just tempt them to use it. The reader insisted that responsible parents teach their teens to operate on a cash-only basis.

The problem with that reader's thinking is that we live in a world where a credit card is sometimes a necessity. For example, consider the travel industry. You can't rent a car unless you have a credit card. A hotel clerk will not guarantee a room for you unless you provide your credit card number. And thanks to terrorists, you can no longer buy an airplane ticket

Many families owe tens of thousands of dollars on their credit cards, and continue to charge their purchases while only making the minimum payments.

with cash because it's not traceable.

It's quite likely that our adult children will be required to travel for their work at times, and will also want to travel for pleasure. They'll need a credit card to do either of those things. Yet we read and hear about many adults whose credit card use has gone out of control. How do we teach our teens to use credit responsibly?

The current high rate of personal bankruptcies makes it clear that our teens can benefit from being taught about credit cards. They need to learn both the advantages and disadvantages of credit card use, and the sooner they learn this, the better. As parents, it's our job to teach them what they'll need to know to handle credit responsibly.

First, we need to look in the mirror:

Are *we* using credit responsibly? Do *we* carry balances?

If so, how can we expect our teens to be financially savvy when we're paying 20% or more interest on all our purchases? Our example speaks much louder than our words.

Next, we should consider at what age we're willing to let our teens obtain a credit card. Should we let them use ours, should we co-sign an account with them, or should we make them wait until they can qualify for their own? Once we make that decision, we'll know how soon we need to teach our teens about credit.

Finally, in addition to explaining the specifics of credit cards and how they work, we must be willing to open up and talk about our financial beliefs and experiences with our teens. It's not easy to admit the financial mistakes we've made, but if sharing those mistakes will prevent our teens from repeating them, it's worth swallowing our pride and being upfront about them.

Of course, it's also important to share our successes, so that our teens realize how we have benefited from wise financial decisions, and that they can, too.

In teaching our teenagers about financial matters, both formally and by example, my husband and I emphasized the importance of building up savings, and having a goal of being debt-free. But we also taught them how credit cards work, what the dangers are, and that if they used them, they should pay them off each month.

When it came to actually obtaining credit cards, however, they were on their own. We didn't want to co-sign an account, nor did we want them using our credit cards, which we use only occasionally anyway. As it worked out, they all obtained credit cards in their late teens without our help; once teens turn 18, they don't need their parent's signature to get a credit card (or several of them!)

Young people in their mid-teens can get a head start on establishing a good credit rating. Opening a checking account, keeping it balanced, and never bouncing checks or creating overdrafts with a debit card are good first steps. (Using a debit card will also get your teen in the habit of looking at plastic as having a limit, i.e. the amount in the checking account. That helps to train their thinking so that once they get credit cards, they don't think of them as "limitless." That's how people end up with $15,000 credit card balances!)

Another good way for a teen to establish credit is to apply for a cellular phone account in his or her name. Some companies will allow an older teen to put down a deposit of a few hundred dollars, from which the first few months' bills will be deducted. After that, the teen will be billed monthly. A pattern of regular, on-time payments will lay the foundation for establishing an excellent credit rating.

If your teen plans to attend college, both of you should be aware that the credit card industry has become increasingly predatory towards teenagers in recent years. At colleges, registration day often includes display tables of credit card companies offering a free pizza or pitcher of beer for any student who turns in a completed credit card application. Young people fill out these applications just to get the freebie, but later on in the year, when there's more semester left than spending money, the credit card will tempt students to spend what they do not have. Many students graduate from college with thousands of dollars of credit card debt in addition to an increasing student loan burden.

Educate your teenager about credit cards with the activities that start on the next page.

Assignment:

___ Save a credit card offer you receive in the mail and examine it with your teenager. Point out and explain the following:

- the annual percentage rate being offered (explain that this may go up at any time)
- the annual fee (if there is one)
- the grace period
- the credit limit
- the kind of information required to apply (income, credit references)
- find a vanity card offer (usually signified by the word "gold" or "platinum" in the name), and detail its advantages, if there are any.

Make very clear to him that this is not free money; it must be paid back. If repaid within the grace period, there will be no interest charge. But if he carries a balance by paying only the minimum payment each month, he will be paying interest on top of the purchase price of everything he charges to that card.

___ Now dig out of your files (or piles) one of your own credit card statements, preferably one with a large purchase on it. Compare the amount of the total purchase with the minimum payment, noting the difference between the two.

For example, a recent credit card statement of mine showed a purchase total for that month of $1,693.14, yet the minimum monthly payment required was only $34.00. It would take over four years (50 months) to repay $1,693.14 at a rate of $34.00 each month, if there were no interest being charged on the balance. Unfortunately, that's not the case. The card charges an annual interest rate of 14.99%.

In addition, suppose I added more purchases to that balance the next month? The minimum payment would increase a small amount, but the balance would increase far more. Repeat this on a monthly basis, and you can see how consumers get into credit trouble.

___ Go over the figures from the previous step with your teenager and emphasize how important it is to use credit responsibly. I taught my teens to pay off the balance every month, pointing out that then, instead of going into debt, they will actually get free use of the credit card company's money for one month.

___ Your teenager should page through the newspaper, especially the weekend editions, for advertisements that showcase the monthly cost of the item in far bigger type than the total cost. Ads for appliances frequently use this approach. If he can't find it anywhere else, tell him to try the automobile advertisements. Ask him why the advertiser chose to highlight $483 per month instead of the total price of $33,188. (These are the average car payment and car price for 2016, by the way.)

___ Require your teenager to keep a log of everything he spends in one month. At the end of the month, he should total his expenditures. Ask him how he would like to be presented with a bill for that amount right now, which is what would have happened if he had charged everything he bought in the last month. He should then calculate 2% of that amount (the minimum payment) and deduct it from the total. That leaves the balance; ask him how long it would take him to pay back that amount if he had to pay an annual interest rate of 21% on it. Point out that any purchases he makes in the coming month will drive up that balance.

___ Using that same log, ask him to calculate how many of the things he bought last month are still giving him enjoyment, and how many have been long-since forgotten. Explain that many things we purchase provide short-term enjoyment, but if we charge them, we will still have to pay for them long after they cease to make us happy.

___ Assign one-page essays on the following topics. (Research can be done on the Internet, or by using *The Reader's Guide to Periodical Literature* at the public library. Recent material should be used.):

- ◆ How to establish good credit
- ◆ What are credit scores/ratings?
- ◆ Bankruptcy: what it is, why bankruptcy rates are going up, and how it affects us all as consumers.
- ◆ Preventing identity theft and credit card fraud

Assignment continued:

___ Go over the advantages of using a credit card responsibly and establishing good credit:

- ◆ Ease of ordering over the phone and online.
- ◆ A credit card company will usually go to bat for you in disputes over merchant errors.
- ◆ Credit cards are safer than debit cards; a credit card company will usually cover all losses if you report card number theft right away, but banks may not cover all funds stolen if someone uses your debit card number; it depends on how quickly you report the loss.
- ◆ You can't rent a car or buy a plane ticket without a credit card.
- ◆ American Express cards must be paid off each month, preventing a balance build-up.
- ◆ If you use a credit card responsibly, you establish the good credit record you'll need someday to obtain a car loan or mortgage.

Reading assignments

___The first five chapters of *Debt-Proof Living,* by Mary Hunt, which make an excellent case for avoiding credit card debt.

___Chapters 11 to 12 of *Invest in Yourself: Six Secrets to a Rich Life*, by Marc Eisenson, Gerri Detweiler and Nancy Castleman. Chapter 11, "Invest in Your Debts," explains how to pay off debts and earn a high rate of return by saving the often exorbitant interest you would have paid. The authors expose the advertising techniques that encourage people to get into consumer debt, and consider both sides of the debate regarding investing money in traditional ways versus paying off consumer debt.

___Chapter 12, "Your Future is *Not* in Plastics," gets specific about the dangers of credit cards, and how to use them responsibly. Since teenagers are currently being targeted by credit card companies, reading this chapter will prepare your teenager for the onslaught.

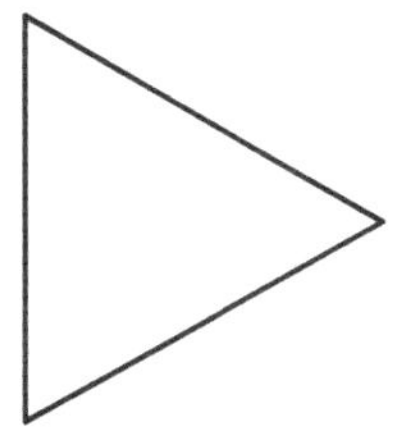

Living Expense Projects

The Rent Project

Background:

Renting an apartment is the dream of many a teenager. Free of his parents' rules, he'll be able to do what he wants, have plenty of space for all his stuff, have friends over at all hours--you may already know this speech by heart. But even if your teenager is not the intrepid, independent type, he still should know what's involved in renting a place to live.

Assignment:

For this project, your teenager should:

___ Look in the classified ad section of one or more local newspapers (your public library will have them if you don't) or on Craig's List (www.craigslist.org) to determine the range of rents for:

- a one-bedroom apartment
- a single or private room in a house
- a small house

in each of these areas:

- your town
- a nearby town
- the nearest large city

___ Call on a few of the local classified ads to find out:

- the amount of security deposit required
- what length lease is required
- the penalty for late rent payment
- the apartment's amenities
- whether utilities, laundry facilities, and parking are included

Assignment continued:

___ Using the information obtained from calling the ads in the previous step, make a simple chart like this one:

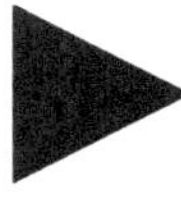

One-Bedroom Apartment Comparison Chart

	Rent 1 Bedroom	Lease Amount	Security Deposit	Late Rent Penalty
In Town				
Nearby Town				
Nearest City				

___ Make a similar chart for the single/private room:

Single/Private Room Comparison Chart

	Rent Single/Private	Lease Amount	Security Deposit	Late Rent Penalty
In Town				
Nearby Town				
Nearest City				

___ Make a similar chart for the small house rental:

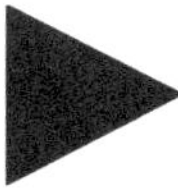 ## Small House Rental Comparison Chart

	Small House Rental	**Lease Amount**	**Security Deposit**	**Late Rent Penalty**
In Town				
Nearby Town				
Nearest City				

Note to parent: comparing these charts should give your teenager an idea of what kind of money it will take to obtain his independence.

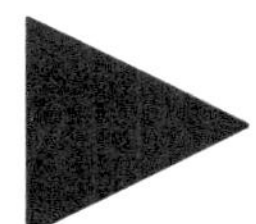 ## For Further Study

Some teenagers have plans to eventually move to another state, one that sounds more intriguing than where they currently live with their parents. If that's the case with your teenager, give him this assignment:

___ Using an Internet search engine, locate the Web site of your chosen town's local newspaper. Using the classified ads there, obtain the rental information you now know you need (rent, lease amount, security deposit and late rent penalty), and add another row to the first chart in this project. Now compare the costs of renting a place in your chosen town to those where you live now.

If you cannot access the Web site of the newspaper in your chosen town, try using www.craigslist.org, or type the name of the town and the phrase "rental apartments" into a search engine.

The Food Expense Project

Background:

Cooking for one is not as cheap or easy as it sounds. After finishing this project, your teenager will realize how much it will cost to keep himself well-fed once he's on his own.

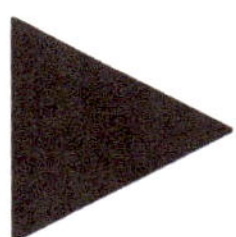

Assignment:

Your teenager should:

___ Make a menu for one week, using his favorite foods, and items he always wanted that you wouldn't allow (pizza for breakfast?). Overall, it should be nutritionally balanced. He should plan three meals a day, with the lunch being something portable he can take to work. He should include snacks.

___Ask you to check his menu to make sure it is nutritionally sound. If he is not clear on the concept of nutrition, you might want to give him a food pyramid refresher course.

___ Make a grocery list of all food items (in the proper quantities) needed for a week's worth of meals.

___ Take that list to the grocery store and write down the price of each item (see page 108).

___ Total the cost of the items and add sales tax, if applicable. Then he should multiply that total by four, for a monthly food expense total.

___ Save this food expense estimate for the Budgeting Project.

Hopefully, your teenager participates in meal preparation for your family. If not, what are you waiting for? Include him in your meal preparations, with a goal of his being able to prepare a meal for your family unassisted, and within your budget. Wouldn't you like a night off from cooking?

▶ **For Further Study**

Have your teenager take the list on page 108 to a local quick-mart or gas station grocery and to his favorite fast-food restaurants. A comparison of the three totals will help your teenager draw some conclusions about the best (and worst) places to buy food, and how much convenience costs.

 **For Further Study**

Grocery List Comparison Chart

Breakfast	Grocery Store	Quick-Mart	Fast Food
Lunch			
Dinner/Supper			
Total			

The Utilities Project

Background:

Utilities are necessities. Utility expenses must be included in any estimate of how much it costs to live in a given place. While we may not enjoy writing big checks each month for services we've already used, that's the price we pay for living in a comfortable home. Your teenager has probably taken the utilities you've paid for all these years for granted. Now is the time for her to learn just what it costs to maintain a comfortable room temperature, running water and enough power to keep her phone and laptop computer charged up.

Assignment:

____ Go through your bill files (or piles) or your online utility accounts and find the past year's paid bills for:

- ♦ electricity
- ♦ natural or propane gas
- ♦ water
- ♦ garbage pickup
- ♦ home telephone

____ Give your teenager access to the paid bills. She should total one year's worth of bills for each utility, and then add them all together to learn how much your family spends on utilities in one year. This can be done on paper or in a Microsoft Excel file.

Assignment:

___ At each utility's Web site, she should find the average usage/cost figure for a one-bedroom apartment. If the information is not offered on the Web site, she will need to call each utility for that information.

___ Water and garbage pickup are usually included with the rent for an apartment, but telephone service is not. Most likely, your teen will have a cell phone and won't need a landline. Otherwise, she should call your local telephone service provider and ask for the average cost of setting up and maintaining a phone line. She may need to be persistent, as phone companies often see customer requests as opportunities to sell nonessential services to their customers.

___ She should save these utility cost estimates for the Budgeting Project.

The Budgeting Project

Background:

Note: in order to complete Part 2 of this project, your teenager should have already completed the Rent, Utilities and Food Expense Projects.

This project would benefit an awful lot of adults, much less teenagers. In fact, it should be required for most states and federal agencies, as living within a budget is apparently a foreign concept to them. Part 1 of this project will take some time, so you might want to assign it a few months ahead of Part 2.

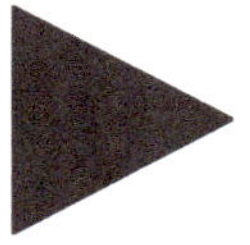 Assignment: Part 1

___ This will require diligence on your teenager's part. For two to three months, she should write down everything she buys, and each item's cost. A brief description of each expenditure will suffice, as long as it gives her an idea of how to categorize the expense. For example:

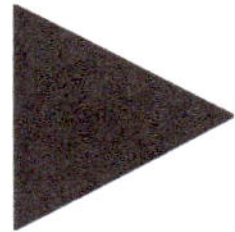

        June 1- clothes- $35
                movie, pop and popcorn- $14
        June 3- magazine- $5
                candy bar- 79¢
        June 4- DVD- $17
                gasoline- $12
        June 5- church offering- $5

During the same time period, she should keep a separate list detailing every bit of income she takes in, whether from a paycheck, allowance, babysitting or lawn-mowing money, or cash gifts.

Assignment continued:

After doing this for two or three months, your teenager should total her expenses by category. This doesn't have to be too complicated. Some good category headings include:

- ◆ clothes
- ◆ entertainment
- ◆ food/snacks/dining out
- ◆ cell phone (if she pays for her own)
- ◆ transportation
- ◆ giving/charity
- ◆ personal items/toiletries
- ◆ miscellaneous
- ◆ savings

Now she should:

___ Total the categories for a total expense figure.

___ Divide the total of each expense category into the total expense figure in order to determine what percentage of her expenses comes from each category.

___ Use these figures to make a simple pie chart, which will illustrate just where her money goes.   Example:

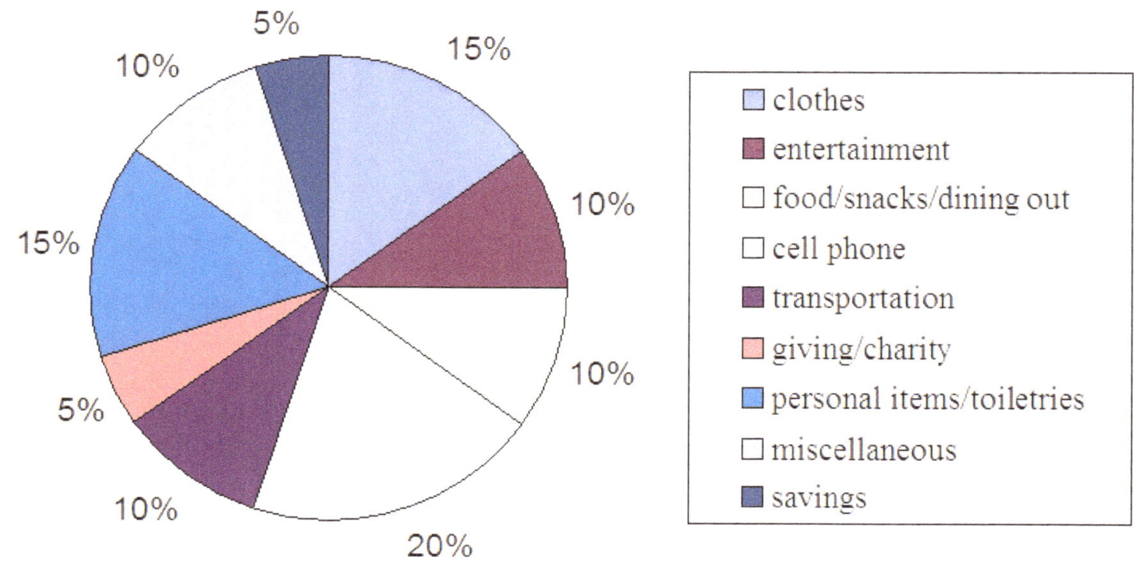

___ Total all the money she took in during the same time period. How does it compare to what she spent? Was she able to save some of it?

Parents:

Going over these figures with your teenager will provide an opportunity for discussion about living within one's means. Tell your teenager that how she spends her money is a reflection of what her values are. If you see areas where she needs help in setting priorities, now is the time to talk about them.

Assignment: Part 2

___ List the following expenses, as calculated in the Rent, Utilities, and Food Expense Projects. If your teenager's future plans include living in a city with public transportation, she needn't add the figures from the Car Projects. Otherwise, they should also be included.

Monthly rent: ______________

Average monthly utility cost: ______________

Average monthly food cost: ______________

Monthly car expense (optional): ______________

Total: ______________

This is a low estimate. Point out that it doesn't include clothes, entertainment or miscellaneous expenses, all of which she learned about in the first step of this project. It also doesn't include charitable giving or savings, both of which are important. It does give her a reality check, so that she has an idea of what living independently will cost.

It also gives her an idea of how much she'll have to earn to live where and how she dreams of living. Do her future career plans correlate income-wise with where she'd like to live? Obviously, none of her plans are carved in stone, but doing a little math as she's done in this project, and those leading up to it, should give her a feel for what she will need to reach her goals.

For instance, if she wants to be a social worker, and live in the trendy (therefore expensive) part of a large city, her research will show her that at least one of those two goals will need to be adjusted. You can tell her that, of course, but she will be more likely to believe it if she does the math herself.

The Mortgage Project

Background:

If you own the home you live in now, or if you have ever owned a home in the past, surely you recall the closing. On that day, you probably signed more papers without knowing what you were signing than any day before or since. Why is it that we will scrutinize the agreement we sign to obtain a grocery store "supersaver's card," yet we'll blithely sign dozens of mortgage documents we don't understand in order to plunge ourselves into more debt than our annual income?

Did you realize what a commitment you were making on that day? You promised to repay far more than you borrowed, over a period of decades. If, over the course of 15 or 30 years, you missed just a few monthly payments, you'd be out on the street with your credit rating ruined.

Taking on a mortgage is a serious proposition. Considering how likely it is that your teenager will have at least one mortgage during her adult life, shouldn't she know what's involved in a mortgage? Here's your chance to enlighten her. Sit down with her and a copy of your local newspaper's real estate section, or look up your town on www.realtor.com. Then give her the following assignment:

On that day, you probably signed more papers without knowing what you were signing than any day before or since.

Assignment:

____ Study the photos in the real estate companies' advertisements. Choose a condominium, town home or small house in your area, something appropriate for a young adult on her own or a young married couple. This means no 10-acre horse farms, or penthouse condominiums on the lakefront of a major city. Cut out or print the ad and put it in a file folder.

Assignment continued:

____ Now find a few mortgage company, bank or credit union advertisements. Note the prevailing rates and jot down the average rate for both 15- and 30-year mortgages.

Define:

- ◆ Down Payment
- ◆ Points
- ◆ Principal
- ◆ Interest
- ◆ Mortgage
- ◆ Amortization
- ◆ Interest rate
- ◆ Length of Mortgage
- ◆ Closing
- ◆ Property Taxes
- ◆ Title

____ Using a mortgage calculator, work out the monthly payment (principal and interest) for each mortgage, and jot down those figures, including the amount of the down payment used for the calculations. You can go to most real estate Web sites and use theirs, plugging in your figures. You can also find a good mortgage calculator at:

www.bankrate.com/calculators/mortgages/mortgage-calculator.aspx

If you do not have a computer available to you, go to your public library, ask the reference librarian for a book of amortization schedules, and photocopy the applicable page(s).

____ Look at the online listing for the property and write down the listing's annual property tax, as well as any special association or maintenance fees. You can also get that information by calling the listing realtor of the chosen property. Explain that this information is needed for a school project. Thank the realtor for her time.

___ Call one of the mortgage companies, banks or credit unions and ask for the average closing costs involved in obtaining a mortgage. Jot down those figures. Ask the mortgage officer how her company determines if an applicant is a good risk for a mortgage. Thank the mortgage officer for her time.

___ Total the down payment, closing costs, and points. This is what it will cost to get into the home.

___ Call your parents' insurance agent (the one who handles their house insurance), explain that you're working on a school project, and ask for the approximate annual cost of insuring the home or condo. The agent will need to know the location of the home, and its approximate age. Jot down the annual insurance cost. Thank the agent for her time.

___ Make a worksheet similar to this:

__________	Monthly payment (principal and interest)
+ __________	One-twelfth of the annual home insurance cost
+ __________	One-twelfth of the annual property tax
+ __________	Monthly association and/or maintenance fee (if applicable)
= __________	Total monthly house payment

This will be the monthly payment for the length of the mortgage. Skipping payments will result in losing the home, and all the money invested into it (the down payment plus the principal paid down since the inception of the loan).

Reading Assignment

Invest in Yourself: Six Secrets to a Rich Life by Marc Eisenson, Gerri Detweiler and Nancy Castleman

Chapter 13, "Your Mortgage is a Great Investment," includes a brief explanation of what's involved in choosing a good mortgage, and a plug for prepaying it.

For Further Study

___ Research adjustable loans, and determine their advantages (including a lower rate, therefore a lower monthly payment) and disadvantages (the rate, and therefore the monthly payment, can go up).

___ Print out or use the photocopy of the amortization schedule mentioned on page 116 and figure out just how much the mortgage is costing over 15 or 30 years (A), compared to the original price of the house (B). Determine exactly how much interest is being paid to the mortgage company over that time period by subtracting B from A.

___ Research the tax deductibility of mortgage interest. Compare the amount of tax saved through deducting mortgage interest with the annual amount spent on mortgage interest.

___ Highly recommended: Obtain a copy of *A Banker's Secret* by Marc Eisenson. This little book is packed with valuable information about saving money on mortgages. He explains how and why you end up paying two or three times the original price of a home by the time you pay off the mortgage, and how you can keep that extra money for yourself by prepaying a small amount every month. (Parents may learn a few things from this book, too.)

___ Compare the total monthly payment for the property to the rent charged for a similar property in a similar area. Discuss the differences between renting and owning a home.

For Further Study continued:

___ Research the housing crash of 2008, when many people found themselves unable to move because they owed more on their houses than they were worth.

If you own your home:

___ Tell your teenager your current house payment and annual property tax. Compare your home's current value to what you paid for it. Explain the investment value of a home, and why you own a home instead of renting it from someone else.

___ Dig out your mortgage papers, and show them to your teenager. Explain the ones you understand, and examine together those you still don't understand.

If you rent your home:

___ Explain the advantages of renting a home over buying it.

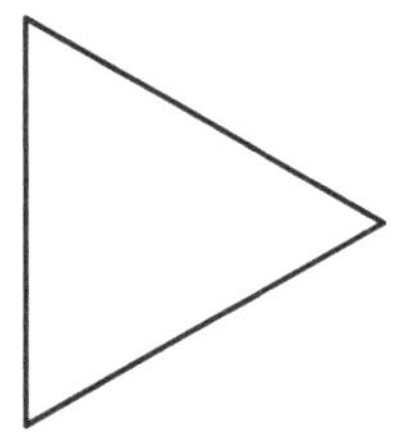

The Insurance Projects

The Insurance Projects

Background:

Teaching your teenager about insurance isn't the most exciting thing in the world, but it's a necessity. In this section, your teenager will learn about car, renters, homeowners, life and health insurance.

Assignment:

Read the following:

Insurance is a product you buy to protect yourself against loss:

- You buy car insurance so that your car will be repaired if it is damaged, or someone else's car will be repaired if you damage it.

- You buy renters insurance so that your belongings will be replaced if someone breaks into your apartment and steals them, or if there is a fire or storm that destroys them.

- You buy homeowners insurance so that your home and its contents will be replaced in case of theft, fire or natural disaster.

- You buy life insurance so that your loved ones will be given money if you should die.

- You buy health insurance so that your medical bills will be paid if you become ill.

It's important to realize that you cannot prevent every single negative event that could happen to you in this life, nor will you need insurance for every little thing that might happen.

These are very general definitions of the most common types of insurance. You may or may not have to buy all of them in the future. However:

♦ If you live in a state where car insurance is required, you'll have to buy it if you want to drive.

♦ Renters insurance is usually optional but is a very good idea if you have nice furnishings and belongings. In some cases, your landlord may require proof of renters insurance before letting you move in.

♦ Homeowners insurance is required by mortgage companies because they hold the mortgage on the house, so it would be a loss to them if the house were to be destroyed by fire or natural disaster. After you pay off your mortgage, you aren't required to have house insurance, but it's a good idea to have it for your own protection. Otherwise, if your house burns down, you may not be able to afford to rebuild it.

♦ Life insurance is usually not necessary unless you have children depending on your income, although anyone can buy life insurance.

♦ Health insurance is usually a necessity given the high cost of medical care, but your employer may offer it at a reduced cost, or if you're really fortunate, as part of your salary.

Here's a simplified explanation of how insurance works: People pay the insurance company monthly or yearly to have insurance. The money they pay (premiums) goes into a pool toward paying claims if/when the problem the people are insuring themselves against happens. Since not everyone will have a claim every day or even every year, there is usually enough cash coming in to the insurance company to cover the claims, pay the insurance company employees and leave a profit.

Some insurance salespeople would have you believe that you'll need plenty of every type of insurance. However, this is not necessary. Which types of insurance you will need depends on a variety of factors. Your budget will be the primary factor, because insurance is not cheap.

It's important to realize that you cannot prevent every single negative event that could happen to you in this life, nor will you need insurance for every little thing that might happen. But you *can* be prepared for such things by keeping a small emergency fund to cover the cost of minor car problems or small medical bills. This will also reduce your insurance costs.

Renters insurance and homeowners insurance are fairly basic products that don't need a lot of explanation; you just fill out a form and the insurance company takes care of the rest. You usually pay for it annually or biannually.

Life insurance is a little more complex because there are two main types: *term insurance* is cheaper and only offers a payout if and when you die, while *universal life* is insurance combined with an investment vehicle. But the bottom line is that if you die, life insurance provides some income to those who are dependent on your income. So it makes sense to buy life insurance once you have dependent children or even a stay-at-home spouse. But until you reach that point in your life, life insurance is not necessary.

You'll learn more about car and health insurance in the next two projects.

The Car Insurance Project

Background:

Here's where your teenager discovers that the cost of his dream car goes beyond the purchase price. The basis of this project is an interview of your car insurance agent. Yes, your teen can easily get a quote online. But it's good for teens to practice their conversational skills by talking to adults.

Assignment:

___ Show your teenager a copy of your latest car insurance bill. Explain the purpose of car insurance, and why you require that he has it, and (if applicable) why your state requires it.

___ Explain the following terms, or have him look up the definitions in a dictionary or online, and have him make a simple glossary with the definitions:

- Claims
- Policy declarations
- Deductible
- Vehicle Identification Number (VIN)
- Premium
- Automobile liability
- Uninsured motorists insurance
- Auto collision insurance
- Auto comprehensive insurance

___ He should list the following information on a sheet of paper:

- Make, model, year and mileage of his chosen vehicle (see Car Project on page 133)
- Safety feature information (antilock brakes, passive restraints, etc.)
- Likely annual mileage he would add to the vehicle
- How many miles he would drive to work or school (one-way)

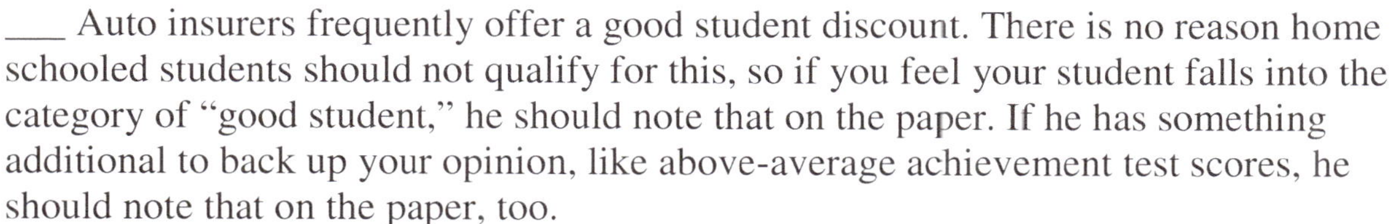

___ Auto insurers frequently offer a good student discount. There is no reason home schooled students should not qualify for this, so if you feel your student falls into the category of "good student," he should note that on the paper. If he has something additional to back up your opinion, like above-average achievement test scores, he should note that on the paper, too.

___ Give your teenager the name and phone number of your auto insurance agent. He should call the agent, introduce himself (mentioning that you are a customer), and explain that he is doing a school research project about car insurance, and would like to ask a few questions. (If it is not a convenient time, he should ask when to call back.) Most agents should be cooperative; after all, this could result in more commissions for them. Your teenager should ask the agent how much it would cost to insure his selected vehicle for six months. The agent will ask for specifics, the answers to which your teenager has already listed on the sheet of paper mentioned earlier. The agent will also want to know whether your teenager will be on his own policy or yours, and will most likely recommend that he be on yours, as insurance companies generally offer multiple car discounts.

___ Once the agent has provided an estimated premium, your teenager should note that on his paper. He may also want to ask the agent for:

- ♦ Recommendations for safe cars for teenagers
- ♦ Models or types of vehicles to avoid
- ♦ Whether old cars need comprehensive and/or collision insurance

Once his questions are answered, he should thank the agent for his/her time. Note: He will need the estimated premium for use at the end of the Car Projects.

The Health Insurance Project

Background:

Health insurance has become increasingly complex. Nevertheless, your teenager needs to understand what it is and why it is necessary, because these days, facing a medical emergency without insurance can easily wipe you out financially.

At the time of this writing, the future of the Affordable Care Act (ACA) is in jeopardy. No one knows whether it will be replaced, or with what it might be replaced. Your best bet is to teach your teen the basics of health insurance so she will have a cursory knowledge of the subject.

You will need the most up-to-date information you can find. Whether your health insurance is provided by an employer, or you obtained health insurance on your own, track down the most recent copy of your health plan and review it before starting this project.

Note: The ACA allows dependents up to the age of 26 to stay on their parents' health insurance policy. Since we don't know if that will continue to be the case, make sure your teen understands the basics of health insurance now.

Assignment:

____ Explain the following terms to your teenager, or have her look up the definitions in a dictionary or online, so she can use them to make a simple glossary:

- ◆ Benefit
- ◆ Claim
- ◆ Co-pay
- ◆ COBRA
- ◆ Deductible
- ◆ Dependent

- ◆ Encounter fee
- ◆ Group policy
- ◆ HMO
- ◆ Open enrollment
- ◆ Out-of-pocket costs
- ◆ Pre-certification
- ◆ Pre-existing condition
- ◆ Preferred provider
- ◆ Premium
- ◆ PPO
- ◆ PCP (Primary care provider)
- ◆ Second opinion

___ If anyone in your family has been hospitalized recently, go over the resulting bills with your teenager. Add them up, and have her divide the total (before the insurance company paid its share) by the number of days of the hospital stay, so that she can determine the per-day cost.

___ Have her total your actual out-of-pocket costs (after the insurance company paid its share), divide that figure by the number of days of the hospital stay, and compare it to the per-day cost in the previous step. This should vividly illustrate why health insurance is important.

___ Assemble pharmacy receipts for all the antibiotics and other medicines your family has used in the past year or so. Go over them with your teenager.

___ Show her a pay stub, so that she can see how much was deducted for health insurance. If you're self-employed, show her your health insurance premium bills.

___ If your health insurance plan offers coverage and deductible choices, show your teenager that the premiums drop as the deductibles increase. Make sure she understands that the more expenses the insurance company incurs, the more money the insured pays in premiums. If your plan offers numerous choices, you might want to make a chart together in order to compare the options.

___ If your teenager is currently employed, she should ask her employer for a copy of the health insurance benefits offered to employees. Studying that information will give

Assignment continued:

her an idea of what she will need to do when she eventually signs up for health insurance with an employer. (If her employer allows it, a brief talk with the company's benefits administrator or human resources liaison could prove to be very informative.)

___ Assign a two- or three-page research paper on health insurance. The research can be done using an Internet search engine, or by using recent editions of *The Reader's Guide to Periodic Literature* along with back issues of periodicals at the public library. Recent material should be used, due to the quickly changing issues surrounding health insurance. The finished paper should include:

- ♦ An overview of the purpose of health insurance
- ♦ Many of the terms listed in the glossary (see pages 126-127)
- ♦ Some details about the controversy over health insurance in our country

For Further Study

Assign an additional page to the research paper explaining how socialized medicine works, and contrasting it to the American healthcare system.

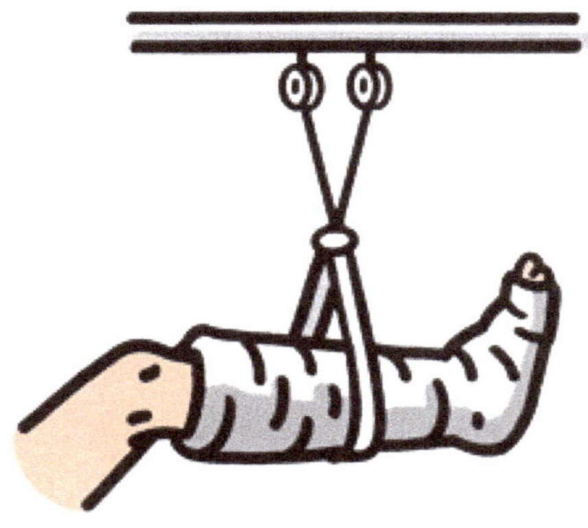

Debt-Proof Living by Mary Hunt

Chapter 20, "Medical Bills Can Give You a Heart Attack," briefly explains health insurance. Only require this if you do not have access to the Internet. Otherwise, you can find something just as informative but more up-to-date online.

If your teenager is work-bound, and if the ACA replacement no longer keeps young adults on their parents' health insurance policies until age 26, find out for certain if your family's health insurance coverage will continue for her once she turns 19. If not, she should call an insurance company and ask for a quote for health insurance for a 19-year-old. (Many employers do not offer health insurance coverage to new employees until they have worked there for a certain period of time. If your teenager has a birthday before she becomes eligible for the employer's coverage, she may need to obtain her own health insurance.) Also, if she chooses self-employment, she will need to obtain her own health insurance as soon as she is no longer covered on your family's insurance.

If your teenager is college-bound, she will most likely be covered by either your family's health insurance or the college's health insurance, at least until she graduates. But depending on your insurance company's rules, and how old she is when she graduates from college, she may need to find her own health insurance after graduation. For now, have her call an insurance company and ask for a quote for health insurance for a 22-year-old.

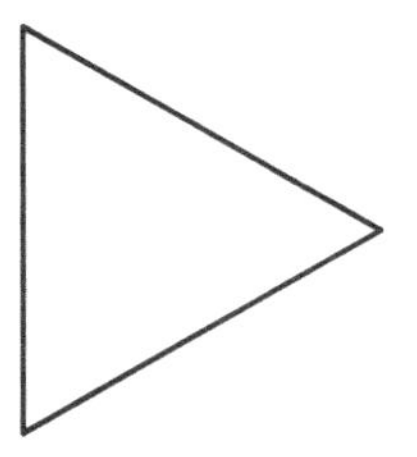

The Car Projects

The Car Projects

Background:

When the urge to buy a car hits your teenager, it will be time to do this project. His interest level will be high, and he will be more than happy to work his way closer to the day he has his own wheels.

The Car Projects are:

- The Car Purchase Project (page 132)
- The Car Insurance Project (page 124)
- The Car Loan Project (page 135)
- Bringing It All Together (page 139)

These projects are most effective when done in order and with one specific car at a time. Your teenager should choose which model to research. Chances are, he already has his eye on one, so use that, unless it's something totally out of the realm of possibility. In that case, have him set his sights a bit lower. This is a reality project, not a fantasy.

If he has no specific model in mind, have him point out a vehicle that appeals to him while you're out driving. Or, if a friend or relative is getting ready to sell a car, and there's a possibility it might end up in your garage, research that model.

For example purposes, we will use a Chevrolet Impala. Since most teenagers have limited resources, and the majority of homeschoolers are single-income families with limited resources, we'll research a used car.

Please note: unless you intend to culminate this project with an actual vehicle purchase, make it clear to your teenager that he is doing this research for educational purposes only.

These projects are most effective when done in order and with one specific car at a time.

The Car Purchase Project

Assignment:

Note: this project requires use of the Internet. If you do not have Internet access, you can find Internet-accessible computers at most public libraries.

Once you and your teenager have decided which car to research, the two of you need to discuss who would be paying for it, and how much money would be spent on it.

____ Your teenager should look through the cars-for-sale section of your local newspaper or shopper and highlight the Chevrolet Impala ads. (The weekend ads usually have the widest variety of models.) He should include any within $2,000 of the price chosen by the two of you.

____ He should highlight those that include the mileage. If none of the ads specify mileage, have him call a few sellers and ask how many miles are on their vehicles. He should take notes, as savvy sellers will mention other features of their cars, and he can use their worth to determine a fair price.

____ Direct him to one of the following Web sites:

- ◆ www.edmunds.com
- ◆ www.autobytel.com
- ◆ www.kbb.com (the official Kelley Blue Book site)

or any other car site that includes a search engine requiring the user to input the model, year, mileage, condition and features of the specific vehicle.

For example, at kbb.com, your teenager should click the "Price New/Used Cars" button on the main page. Then he should input "Chevrolet," "Impala," the year desired and preferred mileage before clicking "Next." The site will ask for your zip code so that it can provide local sale ads for the specific vehicle your teen is researching. (These can be used instead of going through newspaper car ads, if you prefer.)

____ Explain that various features and the mileage on a car are all considered adjustments, which are used when the site computes the prices on the car price estimate (which comes up after he's selected all the options).

___ He should study the estimate. At kbb.com, three prices are listed:

- Dealer price
- Certified Pre-Owned (CPO) from a dealer
- Private party price

Explain to him why there is such a difference between the three prices, as well as the benefits and risks of buying from each type of seller.

___Now that he knows how to do it, he should obtain pricing reports for several other cars he has found in the want ads, so that he can compare them to determine which cars he can afford. This is easily done by filling in a simple comparison chart:

 Comparison Chart

	Year/ Model	Year/ Model	Year/ Model	Year/ Model	Year/ Model
Price					
Mileage					
Option #1					
Option #2					
Option #3					
Option #4					
Seller					

Car Purchase Assignment continued:

By studying the completed chart, he should see that there is not always a direct correlation between age and price, since mileage and options affect the price.

___ Once he starts to favor one specific model, he should do some research so he can learn how that car has been rated by past owners. Ways to determine the consumer rating of a vehicle include:

- ♦ going to a Web site such as www.consumerreports.org
- ♦ going to a search engine and typing in the name of the vehicle and the word "owners" (ex. "Chevrolet Impala owners").
- ♦ going to your local newsstand or your public library and obtaining a copy of *Consumer Reports Used Car Buying Guide* (available in print and eBook versions).

___ Your teenager should scan the car dealer ads in the local newspaper and find the Web sites of several local dealers. Many dealers now list their inventories online, which is very helpful for this type of research. Your teenager should go to each Web site and bookmark those that maintain their inventory lists online. By doing a search of each one's inventory for his chosen vehicle, he will be able to find some for sale nearby. If he is already of driving age, take him to see and test-drive one or more of his chosen vehicles.

___ Once he has found a vehicle that suits him (and you), make sure he has written down the make, model, year, mileage, and safety feature information, because he'll need that for the Car Insurance Project.

___ He will also need the estimated purchase price for use at the end of the Car Projects.

The Car Loan Project

Background:

Note: this project requires use of the Internet.

Even if your teenager is saving up to pay cash for his first car (two of my children bought their first cars with money earned by babysitting), learning about car loans is still a must. Car prices today are incredibly high, and while it would be nice to wait to buy a car until you have the cash saved up, it isn't always possible. If your teenager understands what is involved in borrowing money to buy a car, he will make wiser decisions later on.

Assignment:

___ Explain the following terms to your teenager, or have him look up the definitions in a dictionary. He should make a simple glossary with the definitions:

- Principal
- Interest
- Term
- Rate
- Down payment
- Title
- Co-signer
- Depreciation
- Collateral
- Repossession

___ Using the auto section of your local newspaper, compare the number of car dealer ads that clearly display the total price for each car to the number of ads that promote only the monthly payment (with the total price in the small print). Discuss the reason for this: the dealer is counting on the short-sightedness of a buyer who will look only at whether he can afford the monthly payment.

Car Loan Assignment continued:

____ Explain that the car is actually collateral for the loan, and that the lender retains the title until the loan is paid off. If the loan payments are not made, the lender can repossess the car, since the lender is technically the owner.

____ Explain the concept of a co-signer, and why your teenager might need one. This is a good time to let him know whether you would be willing to co-sign a loan with him.

_____ Using the price of his chosen vehicle (which he determined in the Car Purchase Project), your teenager should deduct a likely down payment, and use the balance to determine monthly payments. First, he should make a simple chart:

 Balance

	1 Year Loan	2 Year Loan	3 Year Loan	4 Year Loan	5 Year Loan
Monthly Payment					

The monthly payments can be determined by using a loan calculator, available at the following Web sites:

- ◆ www.calculatorzone.com
- ◆ www.bankrate.com (click on calculators)
- ◆ www.edmunds.com (scroll down to bottom and click on calculators)

Your teenager can find prevailing car loan rates in the local newspaper's auto section. He can also call your bank, or look on the Internet (rates tend to be lower there). Explain to him that rates can be affected by where he lives, his credit history, whether the car is new or used, and whether he chooses a bank, credit union or automotive financing company.

___ After he notices how much cheaper per month the longer-term loans are, explain to him the concept of depreciation (also, see "For Further Study" on page 138).

___ He should now multiply the monthly payment by the total number of months for the loan to see just how much he would actually be paying for the car in each loan scenario.

12 months × $____________/month = $______________

24 months × $____________/month = $______________

36 months × $____________/month = $______________

48 months × $____________/month = $______________

60 months × $____________/month = $______________

As he notices the increase over time, explain that the additional interest paid on a longer-term loan is like a penalty for the smaller monthly payment.

For Further Study

___ Using the chart on page 136 that compares the monthly payments, have your teenager compute the amount of money he would save by paying off a car loan in two or three years instead of five years.

___ Using his chosen vehicle as the example, and the prevailing auto loan rate as the interest rate, have your teenager fill in the left side of the following chart. (He will need to use a loan calculator).

Comparison Chart

Loan amount: ___________ Interest rate: __________Term: 60 months

	Loan Balance	**Car Value**
after 12 months:		
after 24 months:		
after 36 months:		
after 48 months:		
after 60 months:		

Using an annual depreciation factor of 15%, start with the car's approximate value at the inception of the loan, and determine its value at the end of each year. Fill in the right side of the chart with those figures.

Check to see if there is a point at which the car is worth less than the balance owed. (This is more likely with a new car because the depreciation is so great the first few years, but it could still occur with an older car.) Explain that owing more than a car is worth is called being "upside down" in a loan, and that if a car owner can't make his monthly payment, he can sell the car, but he will still owe money on it.

The Car Projects:
Bringing It All Together

Assignment:

Now that your teenager has some numbers to work with, he should bring together all the information he has gathered by filling out the following chart. After he has determined the total cost of buying and insuring a car, the two of you can discuss whether or not he even needs one yet, and how his future plans (work, college, military service) would be affected by the purchase of a car.

For example, if he's work-bound, having reliable transportation can make all the difference in where he works. But if he's college-bound, and his chosen college does not allow freshman to have cars, he'll have to decide whether it's worth all the trouble and expense of buying a car, only to have to leave it in your driveway for a year while he's away at college.

Chosen vehicle (year, make, model) _______________________

If paying cash for the vehicle:

Estimated purchase price _______________________
Estimated 12-month insurance cost + _______________________
(from The Car Insurance Project on page 124)
Total = _______________________

This gives him a good idea of how much money he'll need to save up for that first car. If he'd rather take out a car loan, he should fill out this chart, too:

If obtaining a car loan for the vehicle:

Estimated purchase price _______________________
Down payment _______________________
Loan balance (purchase price less down payment) _______________________
Prevailing car loan rate _______________________

Monthly payment _______________________
Estimated one-month insurance cost + _______________________
Total monthly cost = _______________________

Reading Assignments

Debt-Proof Living by Mary Hunt

Chapter 16, "Don't Get Taken For a Ride," includes short comparisons of buying vs. leasing, and new car vs. used car, in understandable language. The author recommends paying cash for the best, late-model used car you can find.

Chapter 17, "Every Honest Driver's Toll Bridge," gives a short explanation of car insurance and some tips on claims.

Invest in Yourself: Six Secrets to a Rich Life by Marc Eisenson, Gerri Detweiler and Nancy Castleman

Chapter 14, "Driving a Winner," describes researching and buying a car, and the loan you may need to do so. It includes tables for determining how much you can afford to borrow, and comparing the benefits of rebates to low interest rates. There is also some helpful information about obtaining car insurance.

The Tax
Project

The Tax Project

Background:

Do you remember opening your first paycheck?

The anticipation of receiving the exact amount of money you earned was deflated by the reality of the deductions that had been taken out. This project won't mean much to your teenager until after he has experienced a first paycheck reduced by deductions, so for the most impact, you may want to assign this project soon after he becomes someone's employee.

Assignment:

___ Using his paycheck stub (or one of your own or your spouse's if your teenager is not employed yet), explain to your teenager that:

- ◆ Deductions will be taken from his paycheck so that he doesn't have to come up with the entire amount of income tax owed next April 15th.
- ◆ Deductions will be taken out each pay period; at the end of the year, his employer will total the amounts deducted and report them to him on a form called a W-2 (show him one from your tax files).
- ◆ In the spring, before April 15th, he will need to use a tax form to calculate the tax he owes (show him a 1040, 1040A or 1040EZ from your tax files).
- ◆ He will then compare the tax he owes to what was taken out of his paychecks to see whether or not enough money was deducted during the previous year.

The anticipation of receiving the exact amount of money you earned was deflated by the reality of the deductions that had been taken out.

- If the total amount deducted was more than the tax he owes, he'll get a refund (but only if he files).
- If the total amount deducted was less than the tax he owes, he'll have to pay the balance by April 15th.
- Deductions from his paycheck are taken in order to pay federal, state, and (if applicable) local taxes; separate tax forms must be filed for each.
- When he joins an employer's payroll, he will be asked how many withholding exemptions he wants. The more exemptions he takes, the less money will be deducted from his check. For a teenager dependent on his parents, it's safest to start with 0.

___ Using the tax instruction booklet (also found online at www.irs.gov) and the dictionary, your teenager should make a glossary of the following terms:

- Adjusted Gross Income
- Deductions
- Dependents
- Exemptions
- Itemized deductions
- Form 1099
- Joint filer
- Medicare
- Penalty
- Single filer
- Social Security
- Standard deductions
- Tax preparer
- Wages

___ Your teenager should study the inside cover of the federal tax instruction booklet, where there is an explanation (including pie graphs) of where the federal government gets money from, and where that money goes.

___ Use a copy of your own 1040 form, or a blank one (downloadable at www.irs.gov) to study together. Explain the following, which come from the 2016 IRS 1040 form:

- ◆ Lines 1-5 (filing status)
- ◆ Lines 6a-d (exemptions)
- ◆ Line 7 (wages shown on W-2)
- ◆ Line 37 (adjusted gross income)
- ◆ Line 40 (itemized or standard deduction)
- ◆ Line 43 (taxable income)
- ◆ Line 44 (tax; use the tax table to show where tax is determined)
- ◆ Line 64 (tax withheld as shown on W-2)
- ◆ Lines 75 and 78 (tax overpaid and tax owed)

___ Download a 1040EZ form from www.irs.gov and compare it to a 1040, explaining that teenagers can generally use the 1040EZ.

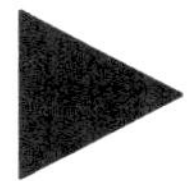

For Further Study

___ Obtain a copy of the United States Constitution, and have your teenager study it to see where it details the fiscal responsibilities of the U.S. government. Then he should compare it to the explanation inside the tax booklet, and determine whether the money he pays in taxes is being used in ways authorized by the Constitution.

___ Assign your teenager a one-page research paper detailing the origin and purpose of Social Security, so that he understands why he has to pay into it out of his paycheck.

___ Assign your teenager a one-page research paper detailing the origin and purpose of Medicare, so that he understands why he has to pay into it out of his paycheck.

For Parents

Part-Time Work for Teenagers

Many homeschooling parents send their teenagers to high school, because the thought of homeschooling through the teen years overwhelms them. Some can't imagine teaching the tougher subjects like chemistry or calculus. Others are concerned that their teens will miss out on football games and the prom. Many just don't think they can handle having teenagers around 24/7.

Those of us who do homeschool our children until age 17 or 18 have fears of our own. In my case, while some of my fears proved to be unfounded, I will admit that homeschooling my teens was quite challenging at times. But the rewards were great, and one of the things I enjoyed most was watching them develop the practical skills that will help them throughout their adult lives.

Teenagers in formal school don't have the time to learn the skills my teens did. School takes over the lives of its students, with its demands on their time not only during the day, but on nights and weekends, too. And it's such an artificial existence, with its bells and its classrooms full of young people all the same age. It's so far removed from real life.

Meanwhile, at home my teens learned the things I wish I'd known how to do before I started out into adulthood. I designed most of the projects in this book for them, and that's how they learned about money, about credit and about loans. They also worked part-time, and then learned to budget their earnings to cover some necessities as well as luxuries.

As a parent, I enjoy seeing my now-adult children use the skills they learned at home. I hope you use the last few years of homeschooling your teenagers to do the same by using the curriculum in this book. In addition, I highly recommend that you encourage your teenagers to work part-time jobs. I believe the skills my teens gained by working were very helpful in preparing them for life on their own.

Unfortunately, the economy has declined quite a bit since my children were teens, so it may be hard for your teens to find part-time jobs in your area. In that case, you may need to use your own personal connections (neighbors, clients, fellow church members, etc.) to find someone to hire them. It will be worth the effort.

Teens Need to Work

I never understood the Poms phenomenon. Why would the parents of teenage girls allow and often encourage them to dress in skin-baring outfits and wave pompoms around while dancing seductively in front of friends, parents and two teams of hormonally-overwhelmed teenage boys?

Then, some time ago, I spoke with a man whose 16-year-old granddaughter had just been chosen captain of her high school's Poms team. We discussed how much time she spent practicing for the tryouts, and how it was an honor at her school to be Poms captain. I asked him if he thought all the time she'd put in was worth it.

"Of course not!" he said. "It's ridiculous. But you have to keep them off the streets and out of trouble somehow, so her parents have always kept her busy with these kinds of things."

I took the lesson of this to be that it's OK to put your daughter on display, as long as you're keeping her busy. Of course, this doesn't just apply to Poms, or just to girls, for that matter. Parents all over America are running themselves ragged trying to keep their teens so busy that they (hopefully) won't have time to get into trouble.

This idea that teens need to be kept busy is a relatively new one. For most of our nation's history, teenagers kept busy by helping their families (first their parents' family, and before long, their own) to survive. They worked on their families' farms and in their businesses. They fought in wars to defend their country. They carved out homesteads across America, fighting Indians, wild animals, and lawless wanderers along the way.

In the early 20th century, teenagers continued to be important contributors to their families. During the Great Depression of the 1930s, many young people worked just to keep food on the table. My father, who was born during that time, was one of four children of a single mother. He began working at age 5, selling gum on passenger trains. By the time he was a teenager, he had landed a job carrying feed sacks at a mill after school each day (and into the evening). The money he and his teenage siblings earned went to their mother, who worked as a telephone operator, to help pay the bills. The five of them eventually pooled their earnings to buy their first house.

Today, most families can survive without relying on the earnings of their teenagers. But that doesn't mean those teens should sit idly by watching their parents work. That's a recipe for breeding laziness and lack of purpose. On the other hand, are parents helping their teenagers by pushing them to try out for Poms, intramural sports, and other activities designed to "keep them off the streets"? In their hearts, surely these teens realize they're being warehoused.

Teens are capable of so much, but they must be given a chance to prove it. Instead of signing them up for activities to "keep them busy," why not encourage them to find part-time jobs? When teens become employees, they learn to get along with customers, follow their employers' instructions, and make good use of their time. These are all important life skills, far more valuable than knowing how to perform a Poms routine.

Benefiting From Part-time Jobs

Homeschooled teens are blessed to have more free time than their formally schooled peers. How they use that time, of course, may or may not be a blessing. It's wasted time if most of it is spent playing video games. But, spent constructively, it can be a real asset to their personal development.

Most homeschooled teens use their free time for hobbies, volunteer work and social activities. While those are all good things, they can be overdone. At some point, part-time paid employment becomes a better use of their time because of all the benefits it provides.

Teens know this instinctively. As they mature, they begin to yearn for the chance to earn and spend their own money. While entrepreneurial types usually start young with lemonade stands and the like, most young people show signs of this desire by their early teens.

A babysitting job or paper route is often a young person's first taste of making money beyond an allowance. Other good "beginner jobs" include dog-walking, yard work, and snow-shoveling.

After the initial thrill of earning money for those occasional jobs wears off, most teens succumb to the lure of the regular paychecks they can earn by working at fast-food restaurants, grocery stores or other local businesses. Such jobs provide a modest but steady income flow that allows them to start dreaming of big-ticket items such as computers and cars.

Homeschooled teens have an advantage over other teens in obtaining part-time jobs because their schedules are more flexible. They can work earlier in the day than those their age who are stuck in a school building until 3 or 4 o'clock. (Be aware, however, that if they're under a certain age, they may not be allowed to work before the local public school's dismissal time. Check with your state's labor department for specifics).

Some homeschooled teens are fortunate to already be part of a family business. They have been learning and earning since they were fairly young. But even these teens can learn something new by obtaining a part-time job away from home. Working for a boss who's not related to you is a lot different than working for your parents.

So for all homeschooled teens, from those who have never worked for pay to those who have been an integral part of the family business, a part-time job can provide money, some independence, and valuable life skills beyond what they have learned at home. When teens become employees, they learn skills they'll need in future jobs, such as:

- ◆ getting along with customers
- ◆ following their employers' instructions
- ◆ making good use of their time on the job

They'll also gain specific skills, from working a computerized cash register to making hamburgers and fries. Then there are the intangible benefits, such as

- learning humility (from having to wear an embarrassing uniform)
- persistence (from sticking with a dull chore like stocking shelves for three hours straight)
- patience (from dealing with demanding customers)
- promptness (from being required to "punch in" on time)

(Admittedly, parents are more likely to view these as benefits than are teens.)

A part-time job gives homeschooled teens something of their own. Those who are being homeschooled along with one or more younger siblings often reach a point where they are tired of doing the same old things. They've been to all the field trips before. They've spent the majority of their waking hours with their family. Now they're ready to do something new, apart from the family.

Some homeschool parents may see that as a bad thing. But we need to allow our teens increasing independence as they work toward that day when they set out on their own. If we look at that process as something that pulls them away from us, we won't be doing them any favors. Instead, we need to encourage them to become independent of us, one step at a time, and enjoy watching them mature. Encouraging them to find part-time work is part of that process

Benefiting from Earning Money

While we parents know that part-time work helps our teens grow into young adulthood, the main attraction of a job from a teen's point of view is the paycheck.

The earnings from a part-time job pave the way for independence and increased self-esteem. The excitement of a teenager who has just bought a new outfit, music system or tablet computer with his or her own money is a sight to behold. Teens also appreciate such purchases far more than if their parents or grandparents bought the items for them.

When my son was a teen, he took a girl from a wealthy suburb to her high school's prom. As a homeschooler, he was curious about what proms are like, and we were curious about what he would think about it. When he returned from the big event, we asked him if he'd had a good time.

"It was fun," he said, "but all the complaining got annoying, especially during the four-hour cruise, when there was nowhere you could go to get away from it."

We asked him what kind of complaining he was talking about.

"The other kids at the prom," he replied. "All they could do was grumble, 'My dad won't get me a better car,' or, 'They never give me enough money!' You can't believe how whiny most of them are!"

I've driven past that high school's student parking lot many times, and have noticed that most of the cars parked there are pretty expensive vehicles. The fact that these teens are complaining about them suggests that they're rather spoiled. As for begging Mom and Dad for more money, it's degrading to be 16 or 17 and have to ask your parents for money all the time, and it's a major nuisance for the parents. That situation can be easily solved by sending the teenager out to find a part-time job.

Teens who earn money learn to make decisions about what to buy, and the money they spend on an item has more value to them because they worked for it. Since they're limited in how much they can earn, they're forced to save up for the things they want. Learning to save is an important skill they'll need once they are adults.

Homeschooled teens are often available to work more hours per week than teens in formal school, but even a few hours of work a week can provide them with many benefits. They can earn their own spending money, buy what they want without pestering Mom or Dad for money, and get a taste of what it's like working in a variety of different businesses.

While the responsibility of getting and keeping a job belongs to your teen, your help may still be required. For example, you may need to drive your teen to and from work, if there are no job possibilities within walking or biking distance of your home. That can be inconvenient, particularly if you still have younger children at home. Just remind yourself that you're providing your son or daughter with one more learning experience, and it's as important as any other subject on that high school transcript.

Helping Your Homeschooled Teen Find a Job

Once it's been decided that your teen needs a job, where should he go to find one?

In a healthy economy, teens can easily find work in stores, fast-food and sit-down restaurants, groceries, movie theaters and bowling alleys. In rural areas, farms and farm stands are good sources of work.

When the economy is good, help-wanted signs make it easy to find a job. In a tough economy, jobs can still be found, but the search will require more effort and thought. Your teen's talents will prove to be an advantage. A musically-inclined teen will have the best chance of working at a local music shop. The young golfer will have an edge when it comes to obtaining a caddying job. An animal lover will want to check out local veterinarians who may be looking for help with their patients.

In most cases, it should be up to your teen to locate a potential employer, and to go through the application and interview process alone.

Here are some ground rules for parents of first-time jobseekers:

- ◆ Don't accompany your teen into the establishment when he goes to fill out the job application.
- ◆ Don't go with your teen to the job interview.
- ◆ Do make suggestions about what to wear (or not to wear) for either event. Appearances are important because they influence potential employers. Your teen might as well learn that now.
- ◆ Remind him to put his phone on 'vibrate' or 'mute' and then put it away; even merely glancing at his phone during the interview is a sure way to turn off a potential employer.
- ◆ Also remind your teen to shake hands firmly, to look the interviewer in the eye, and to ask questions about the job.

That last point is especially important because interviewers are looking for enthusiastic employees. An interviewee who shows interest by asking questions is the first sign that they may have found who they're looking for.

You may want to role-play a job interview with your teen. Be sure to bring up homeschooling in your questioning. The job application will have a blank to fill in with the name of your teenager's school, and a response of "home school" will likely trigger some questions. A confident, patient attitude will go a long way toward calming any biases or fears the interviewer may have regarding homeschooling. On the other hand, if homeschoolers have worked there before, your teen may find that his disclosure actually gives the interview a boost. Many employers say they especially appreciate the work ethic of their homeschooled employees.

Hopefully, your teen's first job application will result in success. But if no interview materializes, or if there is an interview but no job offer, you'll need to take on the role of encourager. There are other jobs out there, and this one might not have been right for him. Let him know that, and then urge him to get back in there and try again. He'll handle the next interview better because he'll know what to expect.

Once he's landed a job, the fact that he got it on his own, without your involvement, will boost his self-esteem and send him to work ready and enthusiastic. And even if his enthusiasm flags after a few days of work, that first paycheck will perk him up again.

Meanwhile, as his parent, you can support him in this without becoming overly involved. You'll need to encourage him after difficult days on the job, be willing to drive him back and forth if necessary, and listen to his stories of cranky customers and demanding managers. After all, his first job will be something he will always remember, and he'll also remember that you helped make that job a reality without doing the hard parts for him.

Answers to Project Questions

The Debt Penalty Project (pages 59-61)
1) $5.00
2) $4.00
3)   3-lb. package
4)   ($12 - $5 = $7)
5) $6.00
6) $2.00

The Debt Calculator Project (pages 62-67)
1) $188.71
2) $1322.74
3) $10,000 principal + $1,322.74 interest = $11,322.74
4) $868.72
5) $1322.74 - $868.72 = 454.02

The Financial Freedom Project (pages 78-79)

1)   They bought a house.
2)   They made $50,000 on it seven years later.
3)   They used that profit to buy their next house, and were able to pay it off early and become debt-free in their 40s.
4)   They both obtained cell phones: Emily's phone cost $40/month, and Caleb's cost $15/month.
5)   The cell phone cost Emily $480/year and Caleb $180/year, so Caleb would come out ahead at the end of the first year by $300.
6)   Caleb saved up cash to put down on it, he bought an older car, and he got on his parents' car insurance policy instead of getting his own.
7)   Emily had already spent all her earnings, so she didn't have any money for a down payment. She also preferred not to drive something as "boring" as Caleb's car, which was all she could afford, even with a car loan.
8)   Emily's car cost $11,000 ($1,000 cash down and $10,000 borrowed). Over the course of four years, she would make 48 monthly payments of $230.29, for a total of $11,053.92. Including her down payment of $1,000, she paid $12,053.92 for an $11,000 car.
9)   Emily paid $40 more per month; over four years, she paid $1,920 more for car insurance than Caleb paid.

10) Caleb chose a local community college, so he could live at home and save both the expense of a four-year school and the cost of room and board. He also chose a career that would only require two years of college instead of four, and yet would be in demand and pay well.

11) Emily chose an out-of-town college, which would cost more for tuition, room and board, and she would have those higher costs for four years. She chose to go there even though her parents could not afford it, and borrowed the money instead. She took her car to college, which would add to her expenses. She also bought a new wardrobe for college and charged it to her credit card.

12) The road trip showed that Caleb had freedom and Emily did not. Caleb had already graduated, and could afford to take time off for a trip before finding a job. Emily had to keep working instead of traveling, because she had so many monthly bills to pay.

13) At 21, Caleb hopes to get his own place, travel to Europe, and eventually buy a house. The chances are good because he has no debt, makes a good salary and demonstrates financial wisdom.

14) No; no.

15) Caleb will be able to, but Emily will not, because she'll have to keep working to pay all of her monthly payments, thanks to the debt she has racked up.

16) Caleb avoided debt where possible, and paid cash for everything. Emily bought and did whatever she wanted, paying for it by putting it on credit.

17) Answers will vary.

18) Answers will vary.

19) Answers will vary.

Appendix A - Book List

A Banker's Secret by Marc Eisenson
Good Advice Press
    Box 78
    Elizaville, NY 12523
    800-255-0899 (M-F, 9-5 EST)
    www.goodadvicepress.com

Debt-Proof Living by Mary Hunt
    Broadman & Holman Publishers, Nashville, TN, 1999

First, Break All the Rules by Marcus Buckingham and Curt Coffman
    Simon & Schuster, New York, NY, 1999

George Muller: Man of Faith and Miracles by Basil Miller
    Bethany House Publishers, Minneapolis, MN, 1941

Getting a Life: Real Lives Transformed by Your Money or Your Life by Jacqueline Blix and David Heitmiller
    Viking Penguin, New York, NY, 1997

Having Our Say: The Delany Sisters' First 100 Years by Sarah L. Delany and A. Elizabeth Delany with Amy Hill Hearth
    Kodansha America, Inc., New York, NY, 1993

How to Be Your Own Selfish Pig by Susan Schaeffer Macaulay
    Chariot Books/David C. Cook Publishing Co., Elgin, IL, 1982

How to Stop Worrying and Start Living by Dale Carnegie

How to Win Friends and Influence People by Dale Carnegie

I Kissed Dating Goodbye by Joshua Harris
    Multnomah Books/Questar Publishers, Inc., Sisters, OR, 1997

Invest in Yourself: Six Secrets to a Rich Life by Marc Eisenson, Gerri Detweiler and Nancy Castleman
    John Wiley & Sons, Inc., New York, NY, 1998

Learn to Earn: A Beginner's Guide to the Basics of Investing and Business by Peter Lynch and John Rothchild
    Simon & Schuster Inc., New York, NY, 1995

Life on the Edge by James Dobson
    Thomas Nelson, Inc., Nashville, TN, 1995

The Millionaire Next Door by Thomas J. Stanley and William D. Danko
    Longstreet Press, Atlanta, GA, 1996 and 2010

Plain and Simple: A Woman's Journey to the Amish by Sue Bender
    HarperCollins Publishers, New York, NY, 1989

Spiritual Investments, Wall Street Wisdom from the Career of Sir John Templeton by Gary Moore
    Templeton Foundation Press, Radnor, PA, 1998

The Templeton Plan: 21 Steps to Personal Success and Real Happiness by John Marks Templeton and James Ellison
    Harper & Row, Publishers, San Francisco, CA, 1987

Ten Golden Rules for Financial Success: Riches I've Gathered from Legendary Mutual Fund Manager Sir John M. Templeton by Gary Moore
    Zondervan Publishing House, Grand Rapids, MI, 1996

The Shaping of a Christian Family by Elisabeth Elliot
    Thomas Nelson Publishers, Nashville, TN, 1992

The Treasure Principle by Randy Alcorn
    Multnomah Publishers, Inc., Sisters, OR, 2001

The Wealthy Barber (updated third edition, 1998) by David Chilton
    Prima Publishing, 1995

Thriving in the 21st Century: Preparing Our Children for the New Economic Reality by Barbara Frank
    Cardamom Publishers, Janesville, WI, 2011

Your Money or Your Life by Joe Dominguez and Vicki Robin
    Penguin Books USA Inc., New York, NY, 1992

Appendix B - Essay Questions

Your Money Or Your Life

Please complete the following essay questions, using facts to back up your answers where necessary. Minimum length requirements follow each question. Please type neatly on separate paper; proof your work.

1) What was the point of the "ham-and-cheese" stories, and how does it fit in with this book? (1/2 page)

2) Define "financial independence". (one paragraph)

3) Does happiness increase with income? Give facts and statistics from the book to support your answer. (1/2 page)

4) Draw the fulfillment curve and label it, then explain it in two paragraphs.

5) In half a page, explain this statement, giving examples:

"Money is something we choose to trade our life energy for."

6) What are the Ten Sure Ways to Save Money? List them, then spend one paragraph describing the one you think would work best and why.

7) What is meant by redefining work? How do *you* define work? (two paragraphs)

8) What are the three pillars of financial independence? Define each. (1/2 page)

9) Draw an example of a wall chart of someone who started with high income and high expenses and ended up financially independent. Take at least half a page to explain what changed from beginning to end, and include an explanation of the crossover point.

10) What, if anything, have you learned from *Your Money or Your Life* that will help you as an adult? If you feel that you haven't learned anything worthwhile from the book, explain how you plan to handle your finances differently. (at least half a page)

 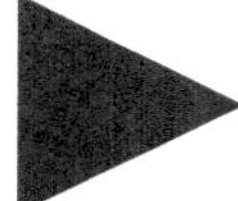

Parents:

Location of answers to essay questions in the book *Your Money Or Your Life:*

1) Pages xxii-xxiii

2) Page xxvi

3) Pages 6-9

4) Pages 23-26

5) Page 54

6) Pages 171- 181

7) Page 230

8) Page 305

9) Page 268 (chart example)

10) Responses will vary.

Also from Cardamom Publishers:

Women of the Old Testament: 14 In-Depth Bible Studies for Teens (with Mother-Daughter Discussion Starters) examines women's stories from the Bible and helps teens relate them to their own and their mothers' lives.

Designed for grades 8-12 and up, this book is arranged in an assignment format, and can be completed in one school year of daily work. The answer key is included for ease of correcting, with specific Bible references for every answer. ISBN: 978-0974218151

Kindergarten Stories and Morning Talks

With this 1890 kindergarten story curriculum, you'll enjoy reading the old-time stories in this collection as much as your child will enjoy listening to them. Originally written and assembled by Sara Wiltse, this book combines familiar stories, many from around the world, with little known and forgotten stories that will make this a favorite book. ISBN: 978-0974218144

Thriving in the 21st Century: Preparing Our Children for the New Economic Reality

Today's children will reach adulthood in an economic environment unlike anything the world has ever seen. The 21st century global economy is powered by an increasing rate of technological change as well as growing foreign competition; both are contributing to the high U.S. unemployment rate and stagnating American wages. How can we as parents prepare our children for success in this growing maelstrom that many are now calling "the new normal"? ISBN: 978-0974218175

These titles and more are available in Books & eBooks from
CardamomPublishers.com,
homeschool catalog companies and many other sellers.

To order more copies of
Life Prep for Homeschooled Teenagers,
please send a check or money order
(U.S. funds only) to:

Cardamom Publishers
P.O. Box 743
Janesville, WI 53547-0743

Number of copies _______________ @ $24.95 per copy ___________________________

Wisconsin residents must pay 5.5% sales tax ($1.37 per copy) _______________

Shipping & Handling ___________________________
($6.65/book for U.S. Postal Service Priority Mail or $3.50/book for 4-7 day Media Mail)

Total = $___________________

(PLEASE PRINT)

Name: ____

Street: _________________________________ City: _____________________________

State: ______________ Zip: _______________ Phone: (_____________) _____________________

E-mail address: ____

In a hurry? Order online at
www.CardamomPublishers.com